THE CITY OF
THE ULTIMATE LOS ANGELES ITINERARY

LOS ANGELES

TRAVEL GUIDE

DIANA L. MITCHELL

© **Copyright 2024 - All rights reserved.**

The content contained within this book may not be reproduced, duplicated or transmitted without direct written permission from the author or the publisher.

Under no circumstances will any blame or legal responsibility be held against the publisher, or author, for any damages, reparation, or monetary loss due to the information contained within this book, either directly or indirectly.

Legal Notice:

This book is copyright protected. It is only for personal use. You cannot amend, distribute, sell, use, quote or paraphrase any part, or the content within this book, without the consent of the author or publisher.

Disclaimer Notice:

Please note the information contained within this document is for educational and entertainment purposes only. All effort has been executed to present accurate, up to date, reliable, complete information. No warranties of any kind are declared or implied. Readers acknowledge that the author is not engaged in the rendering of legal, financial, medical or professional advice. The content within this book has been derived from various sources. Please consult a licensed professional before attempting any techniques outlined in this book.

By reading this document, the reader agrees that under no circumstances is the author responsible for any losses, direct or indirect, that are incurred as a result of the use of the information contained within this document, including, but not limited to, errors, omissions, or inaccuracies.

Cover image: © peeterv / Getty Images Signature sourced from canva.com

Dear reader, thanks a lot for purchasing my book.

To help you plan your trip even more efficiently, I have included an interactive map powered by Google My Maps.

To access it, scan the QR code below.

Happy travelling!

A Note to Our Valued Readers

Thank you for choosing this travel guide as your companion for exploring the world.

I want to take a moment to address a concern you might have regarding the absence of photographs in this book.

As an independent author and publisher, I strive to deliver high-quality, informative content at an affordable price.

Including photographs in a printed book, however, presents significant challenges. Licensing high-quality images can be extremely costly, and unfortunately, I have no control over the print quality of images within the book.

Because these guides are printed and shipped by Amazon, I am unable to review the final print quality before they reach your hands.

So, rather than risk compromising your reading experience with subpar visuals, I've chosen to focus on providing detailed, insightful content that will help you make the most of your travels.

While this guide may not contain photos, it's packed with valuable information, insider tips, and recommendations to ensure you have an enriching and memorable journey.

Additionally, there's an interactive map powered by Google My Maps—an essential tool to help you plan your trip.

I encourage you to supplement your reading with online resources where you can find up-to-date images and visuals of the destinations covered in this guide.

I hope you find this book a helpful and inspiring resource as you embark on your next adventure.

Thank you for your understanding and support.

Safe travels,

Diana

Table of Contents

Welcome to Los Angeles 1
   Why visit Los Angeles? 1
      Iconic Landmarks 2
      Cultural Diversity 2
      World-Class Museums and Art 2
      Hollywood and Entertainment 2
      Culinary Delights 3
      Shopping Destinations 3
      Outdoor Adventures and Beaches 3
      Historical Significance 3
      Vibrant Neighborhoods 4
      Year-Round Attractions 4
Getting Around 5
   Public Transportation 5
      Metro Rail System Overview 5
      Metro Bus System Overview 7
   Taxis and Rideshares 8
      Yellow Cabs 8
      Uber and Lyft 9
   Biking 12
      Bike Share Programs 12
      Best Bike Paths and Routes 13
      Safety Tips for Biking in LA 15
What to See and Do 17
   Iconic Landmarks 17
      Hollywood Sign 17
      Griffith Observatory 18
      Santa Monica Pier 18
      Walt Disney Concert Hall 19
      TCL Chinese Theatre 20

    The Hollywood Bowl 20

    Universal Studios Hollywood 22

    Hollywood Forever Cemetery 23

    Angels Flight Railway 24

    Hollywood Walk of Fame 25

Museums and Cultural Attractions 27

    The Getty Center 27

    The Getty Villa 28

    Los Angeles County Museum of Art (LACMA) 29

    The Broad 30

    Natural History Museum of Los Angeles County 31

    California Science Center 32

    Museum of Contemporary Art (MOCA) 33

    Petersen Automotive Museum 34

    La Brea Tar Pits and Museum 35

    The Grammy Museum 36

Parks and Outdoor Activities 39

    Runyon Canyon Park 39

    Santa Monica Mountains National Recreation Area 40

    Echo Park Lake 41

    Exposition Park 42

    Malibu Beaches (Zuma Beach, El Matador State Beach) 43

    Venice Beach Boardwalk 44

    Los Angeles Arboretum and Botanic Garden 45

    Descanso Gardens 46

    Palisades Park 47

    Kenneth Hahn State Recreation Area 48

Entertainment and Nightlife 51

    Hollywood Nightclubs and Bars 51

    Downtown LA Nightlife 52

    Live Music Venues 53

    Comedy Clubs (The Comedy Store, Laugh Factory) 54

    Theaters and Performance Venues 55

    Casino Entertainment 55

    The Magic Castle 56

    The Echo 57

    The Mayan 58

    The Novo 59

Family-Friendly Attractions 61

    Los Angeles Zoo and Botanical Gardens 61

    Aquarium of the Pacific 62

    Kidspace Children's Museum 63

    LEGOLAND California Resort 64

    Discovery Cube Los Angeles 65

    Travel Town Museum 66

    El Capitan Theatre 67

    Los Angeles Maritime Museum 68

    Underwood Family Farms 69

    Sherman Oaks Castle Park 70

Neighborhood Exploration 73

    Hollywood 73

    Downtown LA 74

    Santa Monica 75

    Venice Beach 76

    Beverly Hills 77

    Silver Lake 78

    Echo Park 80

    Koreatown 81

    Westwood 82

    Arts District 83

Food and Dining 85

    Iconic LA Foods 85

    Street Tacos 85
    In-N-Out Burgers 86
    Korean BBQ 86
    Hot Dogs 87
Fine Dining...87
    Michelin-Starred Restaurants 88
    Internationally Inspired Fine Dining.. 88
Casual Eateries... 89
    Neighborhood Favorites 89
    Trendy Cafes and Diners 89
Street Food and Food Trucks 90
    Classic Street Food 90
    Gourmet Food Trucks 90
Ethnic Cuisine 91
    Little Tokyo.. 91
    Thai Town 92
    Koreatown 92
    Boyle Heights 93
    Sawtelle Japantown 94
Food Markets 94
    Grand Central Market 95
    Smorgasburg LA...95
    The Original Farmers Market.. 96

Welcome to Los Angeles

Welcome to Los Angeles, a sprawling and diverse metropolis that pulses with creativity and excitement. Known as the "City of Angels," LA offers an unparalleled blend of cultures, cuisines, and experiences, making it one of the most captivating cities in the world. Whether it's your first visit or you're a frequent guest, the city's legendary landmarks, eclectic neighborhoods, and rich tapestry of stories provide endless possibilities for discovery and adventure.

Los Angeles is a city of many neighborhoods, each offering its own slice of the LA experience. From the star-studded streets of Hollywood to the bohemian vibes of Venice Beach, the hipster havens of Silver Lake, the historic charm of Pasadena, and the serene coastal beauty of Malibu, every corner of LA has its own distinct personality and allure.

The city is home to some of the world's most iconic sights, including the Hollywood Sign, Griffith Observatory, and the Getty Center. As a global epicenter for entertainment, LA boasts a thriving arts scene with world-class museums, cutting-edge theaters, and legendary music venues. Whether you're hiking in the Hollywood Hills, catching a film at the historic TCL Chinese Theatre, exploring the vibrant street art of the Arts District, or indulging in gourmet food trucks, Los Angeles offers a kaleidoscope of experiences that promise to enchant and inspire.

Dive into our guide to uncover the best of Los Angeles. We'll provide you with insider tips and essential insights to ensure your visit is memorable and uniquely yours. Embrace the glamour, savor the flavors, and soak in the diverse beauty of this extraordinary city. Welcome to Los Angeles—your adventure in the City of Angels starts here.

Why visit Los Angeles?

Los Angeles seamlessly blends glamour, innovation, and a laid-back California vibe, making it a must-visit destination for travelers. Here are some compelling reasons why LA should be at the top of your travel list:

Iconic Landmarks

Los Angeles is home to some of the world's most iconic landmarks. Whether you're snapping a selfie with the Hollywood Sign in the background, enjoying panoramic views from the Griffith Observatory, or strolling along the Venice Beach Boardwalk, these must-see attractions are quintessential LA experiences. Don't forget to visit the Santa Monica Pier, with its historic carousel and vibrant amusement park, for a taste of classic Americana.

Cultural Diversity

LA is a melting pot of cultures, with a rich tapestry of communities that bring their unique flavors, traditions, and festivals to the city. Explore the bustling streets of Koreatown, indulge in authentic Mexican food in Boyle Heights, or visit Little Tokyo for a taste of Japanese culture. The diversity of LA is one of its greatest strengths, offering a global experience within a single city.

World-Class Museums and Art

Art and culture thrive in Los Angeles. The Getty Center, with its stunning architecture and impressive art collections, offers both cultural enrichment and breathtaking views of the city. The Los Angeles County Museum of Art (LACMA) and The Broad are must-visits for art enthusiasts. For a unique experience, explore the street art in the Arts District or visit the Hollywood Museum for a dose of film history.

Hollywood and Entertainment

LA is the entertainment capital of the world. Walk the Hollywood Walk of Fame, tour the legendary studios like Universal and Warner Bros., or catch a film at the historic TCL Chinese Theatre. For live entertainment, the city boasts a vibrant scene with venues like the Hollywood Bowl, the Greek Theatre, and countless comedy clubs showcasing top talent.

Culinary Delights

Los Angeles is a food lover's paradise. From gourmet food trucks serving up innovative dishes to high-end restaurants helmed by celebrity chefs, the city's culinary scene is incredibly diverse. Enjoy farm-to-table cuisine at local favorites like Gjelina in Venice, sample the best tacos at Guerrilla Tacos, or indulge in fresh seafood at Nobu Malibu. Don't miss the chance to explore the bustling Grand Central Market for a true taste of LA's food culture.

Shopping Destinations

LA offers an unparalleled shopping experience. Beverly Hills' Rodeo Drive is synonymous with luxury, while Melrose Avenue is perfect for finding trendy boutiques and vintage treasures. For a more eclectic mix, visit The Grove or the Venice Beach Boardwalk for unique finds and local artisans.

Outdoor Adventures and Beaches

Los Angeles is blessed with natural beauty and year-round sunshine. Enjoy hiking trails in Griffith Park, Runyon Canyon, or the Santa Monica Mountains. The city's coastline offers some of the best beaches in the country, from the lively Santa Monica Beach to the surf-friendly Malibu. The beach towns of Manhattan Beach and Hermosa Beach are perfect for a more relaxed vibe.

Historical Significance

Explore LA's rich history at sites like El Pueblo de Los Angeles, the birthplace of the city, or the historic Olvera Street. The Getty Villa offers a glimpse into ancient civilizations, while the Battleship USS Iowa Museum provides an interactive experience of naval history.

Vibrant Neighborhoods

Each neighborhood in Los Angeles offers something unique. The artistic energy of Venice, the upscale elegance of Beverly Hills, the hipster cool of Silver Lake, and the historic charm of Downtown LA create a mosaic of experiences that make the city endlessly fascinating to explore.

Year-Round Attractions

No matter the season, LA has something to offer. Enjoy summer festivals and beach days, the vibrant fall foliage in Griffith Park, holiday festivities in Downtown LA, and the blooming flowers of spring at the Huntington Library and Gardens.

Los Angeles' unique blend of glitz, culture, and natural beauty makes it a destination like no other. Whether you're drawn by the allure of Hollywood, the culinary delights, the outdoor adventures, or the cultural richness, LA promises an unforgettable experience that will leave you eager to return.

Getting Around

Public Transportation

Los Angeles has a comprehensive public transportation system that helps residents and visitors navigate the city's vast expanse. The Los Angeles County Metropolitan Transportation Authority (Metro) operates the Metro Rail and Metro Bus systems, providing extensive coverage across the region.

Metro Rail System Overview

The Metro Rail system is an efficient and affordable way to travel around Los Angeles, connecting key neighborhoods, cultural attractions, and business districts. The system comprises six lines, with additional expansions underway to improve connectivity further.

Red Line:

- **Route:** Runs from Union Station in Downtown LA to North Hollywood.
- **Key Stops:** Union Station, Civic Center/Grand Park, Pershing Square, Hollywood/Highland, Universal City/Studio City, North Hollywood.
- **Attractions:** Hollywood Walk of Fame, Universal Studios, TCL Chinese Theatre.

Purple Line:

- **Route:** Connects Union Station with Koreatown, extending to Beverly Hills and Century City in future expansions.
- **Key Stops:** Union Station, Pershing Square, Wilshire/Vermont, Wilshire/Western.
- **Attractions:** Koreatown, Wiltern Theatre, future connections to Beverly Hills and Century City.

Blue (A) Line:

- **Route:** Travels from Downtown LA to Long Beach.
- **Key Stops:** Pico, 7th Street/Metro Center, Willowbrook/Rosa Parks, Downtown Long Beach.
- **Attractions:** Long Beach Aquarium, The Pike Outlets, Downtown LA.

Expo (E) Line:

- **Route:** Connects Downtown LA to Santa Monica.
- **Key Stops:** 7th Street/Metro Center, USC/Expo Park, Culver City, Downtown Santa Monica.
- **Attractions:** Santa Monica Pier, Exposition Park, University of Southern California (USC).

Green (C) Line:

- **Route:** Runs from Norwalk to Redondo Beach, intersecting with the Blue Line at Willowbrook/Rosa Parks Station.
- **Key Stops:** Norwalk, Lakewood, Aviation/LAX, Redondo Beach.
- **Attractions:** Easy access to LAX via shuttle, South Bay beaches.

Gold (L) Line:

- **Route:** Travels from East Los Angeles to Azusa, passing through Union Station and Pasadena.
- **Key Stops:** East LA Civic Center, Union Station, Chinatown, South Pasadena, Memorial Park, Sierra Madre Villa.
- **Attractions:** Old Town Pasadena, Chinatown, Little Tokyo.

Metro Rail Services:

- **Operating Hours:** Approximately 5 AM to midnight, with extended hours on weekends.
- **Frequency:** Trains typically run every 10-15 minutes during peak hours, with less frequent service during off-peak times.
- **Fares:** TAP cards are used for payment. A single ride costs $1.75, with free transfers within two hours on a one-way trip. Day passes ($7) and monthly passes ($100) are also available.

Metro Bus System Overview

The Metro Bus system is extensive, covering over 1,400 square miles of the Los Angeles area. With more than 200 bus routes, it connects neighborhoods, business districts, and tourist attractions, supplementing the Metro Rail network.

Types of Metro Buses:

- **Local Buses:** These buses make frequent stops and serve major streets and neighborhoods throughout the city. They are ideal for short trips and provide comprehensive coverage.
- **Rapid Buses:** These buses make fewer stops than local buses, traveling along major corridors to reduce travel time. Look for the red buses marked with an "R."
- **Express Buses:** These buses provide faster service with limited stops, often using freeways to connect distant areas. They are marked with an "X" and are ideal for longer trips.

Key Metro Bus Routes:

- **Metro Silver Line (910/950):** Provides express service between El Monte and San Pedro, with stops in Downtown LA, Harbor Gateway, and other major transit hubs.
- **Metro Orange Line (G Line):** A bus rapid transit route running from North Hollywood to Chatsworth. This line uses dedicated bus lanes to offer a faster and more reliable service.
- **Metro Rapid Lines:** Key rapid routes include the 720 (Wilshire Blvd), 733 (Venice Blvd), and 754 (Vermont Ave), providing quick travel along some of LA's busiest streets.

Metro Bus Services:

- **Operating Hours:** Most routes operate from early morning until late night, with some routes running 24 hours.
- **Frequency:** Local and rapid buses typically run every 10-20 minutes during peak hours, with express buses running less frequently.
- **Fares:** Same as Metro Rail, with TAP cards used for payment. A single ride costs $1.75, with free transfers within two hours on a one-way trip. Day passes ($7) and monthly passes ($100) are available.

Additional Information:

- **Real-Time Tracking:** Metro offers real-time tracking for buses via their website and mobile apps, allowing passengers to check arrival times and plan their trips more effectively.
- **Accessibility:** All Metro buses and trains are equipped to accommodate passengers with disabilities, featuring ramps, lifts, and designated seating areas.
- **Safety:** Metro provides a safe travel environment with security personnel and surveillance systems on board buses and at stations.

The Metro Rail and Metro Bus systems together offer a comprehensive and convenient way to navigate Los Angeles, making it easy to reach key destinations without the hassle of driving and parking. Whether you're commuting, sightseeing, or just exploring the city, Metro's extensive network can help you get where you need to go efficiently.

Taxis and Rideshares

Los Angeles offers a variety of convenient transportation options for getting around the city, including traditional yellow cabs and popular rideshare services like Uber and Lyft. Whether you need a quick ride across town or a comfortable trip to the airport, these services can provide flexible and reliable transportation.

Yellow Cabs

Overview: Yellow cabs have been a staple of urban transportation for decades and remain a reliable option for getting around Los Angeles. Known for their distinctive color and iconic presence, yellow cabs are widely available throughout the city.

How to Hail a Yellow Cab:

- **Street Hailing:** You can hail a yellow cab on the street in busy areas such as Downtown LA, Hollywood, and near major hotels and attractions.
- **Taxi Stands:** Found at major transportation hubs like Union Station, LAX, and popular shopping centers, taxi stands provide a convenient place to find a cab.
- **Phone and Apps:** You can also book a yellow cab by calling local taxi companies or using apps like Curb or Flywheel, which allow you to request a ride, track the cab's arrival, and pay electronically.

Fares and Payment:

- **Metered Rates:** Yellow cabs operate on a metered fare system. The base fare typically starts at around $2.85, with additional charges per mile and per minute of waiting time.
- **Flat Rates:** Some routes, such as trips to and from LAX, may offer flat-rate pricing. For example, a standard flat rate from LAX to Downtown LA is approximately $46.
- **Payment Options:** Most yellow cabs accept cash, credit, and debit cards. The Curb and Flywheel apps also allow for in-app payment, providing a cashless and convenient option.

Advantages of Yellow Cabs:

- **Availability:** Yellow cabs are readily available in high-traffic areas and can be hailed on the spot without needing a pre-arranged booking.
- **Regulated Service:** Taxi companies are regulated by the city, ensuring that drivers are licensed and vehicles meet safety standards.
- **Knowledgeable Drivers:** Taxi drivers are typically familiar with the city's layout and can navigate traffic efficiently, especially in busy areas.

Uber and Lyft

Overview: Rideshare services like Uber and Lyft have become incredibly popular in Los Angeles, offering a convenient and often more affordable alternative to traditional taxis. These services operate through mobile apps, allowing users to request rides, track their driver's location, and pay electronically.

How to Use Uber and Lyft:

- **Download the App:** Download the Uber or Lyft app from the App Store or Google Play Store and create an account.
- **Request a Ride:** Open the app, enter your destination, and choose the type of ride you prefer (e.g., UberX, UberXL, Lyft, Lyft Lux).
- **Track Your Driver:** Once your ride is confirmed, you can track your driver's location in real-time and see their estimated arrival time.
- **Payment:** Payment is handled through the app using the credit or debit card linked to your account. You can also add a tip for your driver through the app after the ride.

Ride Options:

- **Economy Rides:** UberX and Lyft offer affordable rides for up to four passengers, making them a cost-effective option for solo travelers or small groups.
- **Premium Rides:** For a more luxurious experience, options like Uber Black, Uber Lux, and Lyft Lux provide high-end vehicles with professional drivers.
- **Shared Rides:** Uber Pool and Lyft Shared allow you to share your ride with other passengers heading in the same direction, reducing costs and environmental impact.
- **Specialty Rides:** Uber and Lyft also offer options for larger groups (UberXL, Lyft XL) and accessible vehicles (Uber WAV, Lyft Access).

Advantages of Uber and Lyft:

- **Convenience:** With the ability to request a ride from your smartphone and track the driver's arrival, rideshare services offer unmatched convenience.
- **Transparent Pricing:** The app provides an estimate of the fare before you book the ride, so you know what to expect. Surge pricing may apply during peak times, but this is clearly communicated before you confirm your ride.

- **Safety Features:** Both Uber and Lyft have built-in safety features, including driver profiles, real-time GPS tracking, and the ability to share your ride details with friends and family.
- **Flexibility:** Rideshare services are available 24/7, making them a reliable option for late-night trips or early morning airport rides.

Tipping:

- **Yellow Cabs:** Tipping is customary, with a standard tip being 15-20% of the fare.
- **Uber and Lyft:** You can tip your driver through the app after your ride is complete. The suggested tip amounts vary, but typically 10-20% of the fare is appreciated.

Safety Tips:

- **Verify Your Ride:** Always check the driver's name, photo, and license plate number provided in the app before getting into the vehicle.
- **Share Your Trip:** Use the app's feature to share your trip details with a trusted contact for added security.
- **Sit in the Back:** When riding alone, sit in the back seat to maintain personal space and ensure you can exit safely on either side.

Using yellow cabs, Uber, and Lyft in Los Angeles offers flexibility and convenience, making it easier to navigate the city and reach your destinations. Whether you prefer the traditional taxi experience or the modern convenience of rideshares, LA provides ample options to suit your travel needs.

Biking

Exploring Los Angeles by bike can be an exciting and eco-friendly way to experience the city. Whether you're a seasoned cyclist or a casual rider, LA offers a variety of bike share programs and scenic routes that cater to all levels. Here's an in-depth look at biking in Los Angeles, including bike share programs and some of the best bike paths and routes the city has to offer.

Bike Share Programs

Metro Bike Share

Metro Bike Share is a popular program in Los Angeles, providing convenient access to bicycles for both locals and visitors. The program has several docking stations throughout the city, particularly in high-traffic areas and near public transportation hubs.

How It Works:

- **Rent:** Bikes can be rented from one of the many docking stations using the Metro Bike Share app, a TAP card, or a credit card.
- **Return:** Bikes can be returned to any docking station, making it easy to end your ride wherever you need to.
- **Pricing:** Pay-as-you-go rates are around $1.75 for every 30 minutes. There are also day passes ($5 for unlimited 30-minute rides) and monthly memberships ($17 per month).

Locations:

- **Downtown LA:** Numerous stations around popular destinations such as Union Station, Grand Park, and the Arts District.
- **Venice:** Stations near the beach and boardwalk, providing easy access to coastal paths.
- **Expo Line Corridor:** Stations along the Expo Line, offering a seamless transition between biking and public transit.

Breeze Bike Share

Breeze Bike Share, operated by Santa Monica, extends the bike share network to the western part of LA County, particularly around Santa Monica and Venice.

How It Works:

- **Rent:** Bikes can be rented using the Social Bicycles app or a credit card at docking stations.
- **Return:** Bikes can be locked to any Breeze station or public bike rack within the service area.
- **Pricing:** Pay-as-you-go rates are $1 for every 10 minutes. Monthly memberships are also available for $25, including 90 minutes of ride time per day.

Locations:

- **Santa Monica:** Numerous stations throughout the city, especially near the beach, downtown area, and parks.
- **Venice:** Stations providing access to the Venice Beach boardwalk and connecting to Metro Bike Share stations.

Best Bike Paths and Routes

Los Angeles offers a variety of scenic bike paths and routes that cater to different preferences and skill levels. Here are some of the best options:

The Strand (Marvin Braude Bike Trail)

- **Description:** This iconic 22-mile coastal bike path stretches from Will Rogers State Beach in Pacific Palisades to Torrance Beach. It's a flat, easy ride perfect for all ages and skill levels.
- **Highlights:** The path passes through several popular beach destinations, including Santa Monica, Venice, Manhattan Beach, and Hermosa Beach. Riders can enjoy ocean views, beachfront cafes, and lively boardwalks.
- **Best For:** Leisurely rides, beach lovers, family outings.

Ballona Creek Bike Path

- **Description:** A 7.4-mile path that follows Ballona Creek from Culver City to Marina del Rey, offering a mix of urban and natural scenery.
- **Highlights:** The path runs along the creek, providing a serene ride with views of wetlands and wildlife. It also connects to the Marvin Braude Bike Trail at Marina del Rey.
- **Best For:** Nature enthusiasts, commuters, those looking for a peaceful ride.

LA River Bike Path

- **Description:** Runs along the Los Angeles River, providing a scenic and mostly flat ride through the heart of the city. The path is currently being extended to connect more neighborhoods.
- **Highlights:** The path offers views of the river's revitalized areas, public art installations, and green spaces. Key sections include Elysian Valley (Frogtown) and Downtown LA.
- **Best For:** Urban explorers, art lovers, casual cyclists.

Griffith Park

- **Description:** Griffith Park offers several bike-friendly roads and trails, with routes leading to the Griffith Observatory and around the park's scenic areas.
- **Highlights:** The park features lush landscapes, panoramic views of the city, and landmarks like the Griffith Observatory and the Los Angeles Zoo. Trails vary in difficulty, catering to both casual and experienced cyclists.
- **Best For:** Nature lovers, fitness enthusiasts, families.

Expo Line Bike Path

- **Description:** This dedicated bike path runs parallel to the Expo Line light rail route from Culver City to Santa Monica, providing a safe and convenient way to bike between these areas.
- **Highlights:** The path offers easy access to several attractions, including the Santa Monica Pier, Culver City's vibrant downtown area, and various parks. It's ideal for combining biking with public transit.

- **Best For:** Commuters, urban cyclists, those connecting with public transit.

Elysian Park

- **Description:** Elysian Park offers a variety of trails with scenic views of Downtown LA and Dodger Stadium.
- **Highlights:** The park's trails provide a mix of paved and dirt paths, with routes that vary in difficulty. Riders can enjoy the park's natural beauty, picnic areas, and panoramic vistas.
- **Best For:** Outdoor enthusiasts, intermediate cyclists, those seeking a quieter ride.

Safety Tips for Biking in LA

- **Wear a Helmet:** Always wear a helmet for safety, regardless of your experience level.
- **Use Lights and Reflectors:** Equip your bike with front and rear lights, especially if riding at night, and wear reflective clothing.
- **Follow Traffic Laws:** Obey all traffic signals and signs, ride in the same direction as traffic, and use hand signals to indicate turns and stops.
- **Stay Aware:** Be mindful of your surroundings, watch out for pedestrians and vehicles, and avoid distractions like headphones.
- **Plan Your Route:** Use maps and apps to plan your route in advance, opting for bike lanes and quieter streets whenever possible.

By taking advantage of bike share programs and exploring the best bike paths and routes, you can enjoy a unique and active way to experience Los Angeles. Whether you're commuting, sightseeing, or simply enjoying a leisurely ride, biking offers a flexible and enjoyable way to navigate the city.

What to See and Do

Iconic Landmarks

Hollywood Sign

The Hollywood Sign is one of the most iconic landmarks in Los Angeles and a symbol of the entertainment industry worldwide. Perched atop the Hollywood Hills in the Santa Monica Mountains, this massive sign overlooks the city, providing a stunning and recognizable backdrop. Originally erected in 1923 as "Hollywoodland" to promote a real estate development, the sign quickly became synonymous with the glitz and glamour of the burgeoning film industry.

Each letter of the sign stands 45 feet tall, and the entire structure spans 350 feet. Over the years, the sign has undergone numerous restorations, reflecting its enduring significance. It was shortened to "Hollywood" in 1949, and by the late 1970s, it had fallen into disrepair. The Hollywood Chamber of Commerce launched a successful campaign to restore it, funded by notable figures in the entertainment industry.

Visitors can enjoy various viewpoints of the sign, but for those seeking a closer look, there are several hiking trails in Griffith Park that offer fantastic perspectives. The Mt. Hollywood Trail, the Brush Canyon Trail, and the Cahuenga Peak Trail each provide different vantage points and experiences. It's important to note that the sign itself is fenced off to prevent vandalism, but the trails offer plenty of opportunities for breathtaking photos and views of Los Angeles.

The Hollywood Sign's significance goes beyond its physical presence. It embodies the dreams and aspirations associated with Hollywood and has become a cultural icon featured in countless films, television shows, and advertisements. Its enduring appeal continues to attract millions of visitors each year, making it a must-see destination for tourists and a cherished symbol for locals.

Griffith Observatory

[handwritten: $42.00 per person — some options free]

Griffith Observatory, located on the southern slope of Mount Hollywood in Griffith Park, is one of Los Angeles' most popular attractions. Opened in 1935, the observatory offers a unique blend of astronomy and stunning city views, drawing millions of visitors annually. The observatory was a gift from Colonel Griffith J. Griffith, who envisioned a public space where people could observe the stars and learn about the cosmos.

The building itself is an architectural marvel, featuring Art Deco and Greek Revival styles. Its copper domes and white façade are instantly recognizable. Inside, the observatory houses a wealth of exhibits that cater to astronomy enthusiasts and casual visitors alike. The Foucault pendulum, the Tesla coil, and a large collection of meteorites are just a few highlights.

One of the observatory's main attractions is the Samuel Oschin Planetarium, which offers state-of-the-art presentations that explore the universe's wonders. The Zeiss telescope, located in the observatory's east dome, allows visitors to view celestial objects like the Moon, planets, and stars. Free public star parties are held monthly, giving people a chance to gaze at the night sky through various telescopes set up by amateur astronomers.

Griffith Observatory is also famous for its stunning views of Los Angeles and the Hollywood Sign. The observatory's location provides panoramic vistas that are particularly breathtaking at sunset and during the evening when the city lights up. The surrounding park offers numerous hiking trails, including routes to the Hollywood Sign and Mount Hollywood's summit.

In addition to its educational and observational facilities, Griffith Observatory has played a significant role in popular culture. It has been featured in numerous films and television shows, including the iconic "Rebel Without a Cause" starring James Dean. This association with Hollywood further cements its status as a beloved Los Angeles landmark.

Santa Monica Pier

Santa Monica Pier is a historic and vibrant destination that has been a beloved landmark of Los Angeles since its opening in 1909. Located at the foot of Colorado Avenue in Santa Monica, the pier extends into the Pacific

Ocean and offers a plethora of attractions, making it a perfect spot for families, couples, and solo travelers.

One of the pier's most famous features is Pacific Park, an amusement park with a variety of rides and games. The park's Ferris wheel, known as the Pacific Wheel, is the world's first solar-powered Ferris wheel and offers spectacular views of the coastline and city. Other attractions include the West Coaster roller coaster, a historic carousel built in the 1920s, and various arcade games.

The Santa Monica Pier is also home to the Santa Monica Pier Aquarium, operated by Heal the Bay. This interactive aquarium focuses on educating visitors about the marine life and ecosystems of the Santa Monica Bay. It features touch tanks, interactive exhibits, and daily educational programs, making it an engaging experience for visitors of all ages.

Fishing is another popular activity on the pier, with designated areas and bait shops available for enthusiasts. The pier's end offers a scenic spot to cast a line and enjoy the ocean breeze. For those looking to enjoy the pier's culinary offerings, there are numerous restaurants and food stalls serving everything from seafood to classic American fare.

Throughout the year, the Santa Monica Pier hosts a variety of events, including concerts, outdoor movies, and cultural festivals. The Twilight Concert Series, held during the summer months, attracts large crowds with performances from a diverse range of musical genres.

The pier's location also makes it a convenient starting point for exploring the nearby Santa Monica State Beach, which features miles of sandy shores, bike paths, and volleyball courts. The beach is perfect for sunbathing, swimming, or simply taking a leisurely stroll along the shore.

With its blend of historic charm, modern attractions, and beautiful ocean views, Santa Monica Pier remains a quintessential Los Angeles experience. Its lively atmosphere and array of activities ensure that there is something for everyone to enjoy.

Walt Disney Concert Hall

The Walt Disney Concert Hall, located in downtown Los Angeles, is a striking example of modern architecture and a world-renowned venue for classical music. Designed by architect Frank Gehry and completed in 2003, the concert hall is part of the Los Angeles Music Center and serves as the home of the Los Angeles Philharmonic and the Los Angeles Master Chorale.

The exterior of the Walt Disney Concert Hall is instantly recognizable, with its sweeping, stainless steel curves that resemble the sails of a ship. This bold design not only makes it a standout architectural landmark but also enhances the acoustics inside the hall. The interior, with its warm, Douglas fir wood and vineyard-style seating, creates an intimate atmosphere that allows for a close connection between the performers and the audience.

Acoustics are a key feature of the Walt Disney Concert Hall. The hall was designed in collaboration with renowned acoustician Yasuhisa Toyota to ensure that it offers unparalleled sound quality. The result is a space where every note resonates perfectly, making it one of the best concert venues in the world for both musicians and audiences.

The concert hall hosts a diverse array of performances, from classical music concerts to contemporary music events, ensuring there is something for every music lover. In addition to its regular season of performances by the Los Angeles Philharmonic, the hall also features guest artists and ensembles from around the globe.

The Walt Disney Concert Hall is also known for its public art installations and community programs. The exterior gardens, including the Blue Ribbon Garden, provide a serene space for visitors to enjoy before or after performances. The concert hall frequently offers free tours, allowing the public to explore its architectural and acoustic wonders.

Named in honor of Walt Disney, whose foundation provided a significant portion of the funding, the concert hall stands as a testament to the city's commitment to the arts. It has become an iconic symbol of Los Angeles, representing both its cultural heritage and its forward-looking spirit.

TCL Chinese Theatre

The TCL Chinese Theatre, located on the historic Hollywood Boulevard in Los Angeles, is one of the most iconic landmarks in the entertainment industry. Opened in 1927 as Grauman's Chinese Theatre, this famous cinema has hosted countless premieres and has become synonymous with Hollywood's golden age of film.

The theatre's exterior is a striking example of exotic revival architecture, featuring a grand pagoda-like structure, intricate detailing, and two massive guardian lions at the entrance. The elaborate design was inspired by ancient Chinese architecture, and its distinctive style has made it a recognizable symbol of Hollywood glamour.

One of the theatre's most famous attractions is the Forecourt of the Stars, where over 200 handprints, footprints, and autographs of some of the most celebrated actors, directors, and musicians are immortalized in concrete. This tradition began in 1927 when silent film star Norma Talmadge accidentally stepped into wet cement, inspiring the idea to preserve celebrity imprints. Today, the forecourt continues to draw visitors from around the world, eager to compare their handprints with those of their favorite stars.

Inside, the TCL Chinese Theatre boasts a lavish auditorium with a state-of-the-art IMAX screen, offering a movie-going experience like no other. The theatre's opulent interior, adorned with Chinese motifs, chandeliers, and red velvet drapes, reflects the same luxurious aesthetic as its exterior.

In addition to regular movie screenings, the theatre hosts special events, including film festivals, premieres, and celebrity appearances. The TCL Chinese Theatre is not just a place to watch movies; it's a living piece of Hollywood history, where the magic of the movies continues to come alive for visitors and locals alike.

The Hollywood Bowl

The Hollywood Bowl, nestled in the Hollywood Hills, is an iconic Los Angeles amphitheater known for its unique shell-shaped design and rich history of musical performances. Opened in 1922, the Bowl has become one of the most celebrated live music venues in the world, drawing millions of visitors each year. Its distinctive architecture, featuring concentric arches, provides both excellent acoustics and a stunning visual experience.

The Hollywood Bowl is home to the Los Angeles Philharmonic during the summer months and hosts a diverse array of musical acts, from classical concerts to pop, rock, and jazz performances. Its open-air setting allows for an unforgettable experience, where audiences can enjoy music under the stars. The Bowl has also hosted numerous legendary performances by artists such as The Beatles, Frank Sinatra, and Ella Fitzgerald, cementing its status in music history.

In addition to its concert offerings, the Hollywood Bowl provides a variety of cultural events, including film screenings with live orchestral accompaniment and theatrical productions. The venue also supports community engagement through educational programs and free concerts, making the arts accessible to a wider audience.

Visitors can enhance their experience by bringing picnics to enjoy on the terraced seating areas or purchasing food and beverages from the on-site concessions. The Bowl's setting in the scenic Hollywood Hills adds to its charm, offering panoramic views of the surrounding area.

The Hollywood Bowl Museum, located on the grounds, offers insights into the venue's storied past with exhibits showcasing memorabilia, photographs, and recordings. Guided tours are also available, providing an in-depth look at the Bowl's history and architecture.

For over a century, the Hollywood Bowl has been a cultural landmark in Los Angeles, beloved by both locals and tourists. Its combination of top-tier musical performances, breathtaking location, and community outreach make it a must-visit destination for anyone seeking to experience the vibrant arts scene of Los Angeles.

Universal Studios Hollywood

Universal Studios Hollywood is a premier entertainment destination in Los Angeles, combining a world-class theme park with a working film studio. Located in the San Fernando Valley, Universal Studios offers a unique blend of thrilling rides, interactive attractions, and behind-the-scenes tours that provide an immersive experience into the world of movies and television.

One of the main draws of Universal Studios Hollywood is its themed rides and attractions based on popular films and TV shows. Highlights include "Harry Potter and the Forbidden Journey," located in the meticulously recreated Wizarding World of Harry Potter, and "Jurassic World – The Ride," which features state-of-the-art animatronics and special effects. Other popular attractions include "Transformers: The Ride-3D," "The Simpsons Ride," and "Despicable Me Minion Mayhem."

The Studio Tour is a signature experience at Universal Studios Hollywood, offering visitors a behind-the-scenes look at the filmmaking process. The tour takes guests through real sets and soundstages, where they can see iconic locations such as the Bates Motel from "Psycho" and Wisteria Lane from "Desperate Housewives." The tour also includes thrilling encounters with King Kong and Fast & Furious-themed attractions, enhanced by cutting-edge technology.

Universal Studios Hollywood also offers a variety of entertainment options, including live shows, character meet-and-greets, and seasonal events. The WaterWorld show, based on the film of the same name, is a high-energy performance featuring stunts, explosions, and water effects. During Halloween, the park transforms into Halloween Horror Nights, with haunted mazes and scare zones that provide a spine-chilling experience.

Dining and shopping are also integral parts of the Universal Studios experience. The park features numerous restaurants and food stalls offering a wide range of cuisines, from classic American fare to themed eateries like Three Broomsticks in the Wizarding World of Harry Potter. CityWalk, located just outside the park, offers additional dining, shopping, and entertainment options, making it a popular spot for both park visitors and locals.

With its combination of thrilling attractions, behind-the-scenes tours, and immersive experiences, Universal Studios Hollywood provides a unique and unforgettable adventure for visitors of all ages. It remains a top destination for tourists seeking to explore the magic of Hollywood and the excitement of the entertainment industry.

Hollywood Forever Cemetery

Hollywood Forever Cemetery, established in 1899, is one of the most iconic and historic cemeteries in Los Angeles. Nestled on Santa Monica Boulevard, this cemetery serves as the final resting place for many of Hollywood's greatest stars, making it a pilgrimage site for film enthusiasts and history buffs alike. The cemetery spans 62 acres and is not only a place of remembrance but also a vibrant cultural hub.

Hollywood Forever is the resting place of numerous legendary figures, including Rudolph Valentino, Judy Garland, Mickey Rooney, and Cecil B. DeMille. The cemetery's beautifully landscaped grounds and historic mausoleums provide a serene environment for visitors to pay their respects. In addition to its role as a burial ground, Hollywood Forever has become renowned for its cultural events. The cemetery hosts the popular Cinespia outdoor movie screenings, where classic films are projected against the backdrop of a mausoleum, drawing crowds of Angelenos and tourists alike.

The cemetery's annual Dia de los Muertos celebration is another highlight, featuring elaborate altars, live music, and traditional Mexican dance performances. This event honors the Mexican tradition of Day of the Dead, celebrating the lives of the deceased with vibrant displays and community participation. Hollywood Forever also offers guided tours that delve into the history of the cemetery, its notable interments, and the architectural and artistic significance of its monuments and mausoleums.

In addition to its cultural events, Hollywood Forever Cemetery is a designated Los Angeles Historic-Cultural Monument. Its historic chapel and columbarium feature stunning stained glass windows and intricate marble work, reflecting the rich architectural heritage of early 20th-century Los Angeles. The cemetery's blend of history, art, and culture makes it a unique destination, offering a glimpse into the lives and legacies of Hollywood's most famous personalities.

Angels Flight Railway

Angels Flight Railway, often referred to as the "Shortest Railway in the World," is a historic funicular located in the Bunker Hill district of Downtown Los Angeles. Originally opened in 1901, this charming railway has become an iconic symbol of the city, offering a nostalgic ride that connects Hill Street and Olive Street via a steep incline.

The railway was designed to provide convenient transportation for the residents of the affluent Bunker Hill neighborhood, enabling them to travel easily to the bustling business district below. The two funicular cars, named Sinai and Olivet, operate in a counterbalanced system, where one car ascends as the other descends. The ride covers a distance of 298 feet and takes just over a minute, making it a brief but memorable experience.

Angels Flight has seen several closures and restorations over its long history. After operating for nearly 70 years, the railway was dismantled in 1969 to accommodate urban redevelopment. However, due to its historical significance and public demand, it was restored and reopened in 1996, relocated a half block south of its original location. The railway faced another closure in 2001 following an accident, but after extensive safety upgrades, it resumed operations in 2010.

Today, Angels Flight is a beloved landmark and a popular tourist attraction, celebrated for its historical charm and picturesque views of Downtown Los Angeles. The railway has appeared in numerous films, television shows, and literature, cementing its status as a cultural icon. Its orange and black cars, vintage signage, and historic station house offer a glimpse into Los Angeles' past, providing a stark contrast to the modern skyscrapers that now dominate the cityscape.

Riding Angels Flight is not only a convenient way to navigate Bunker Hill's steep incline but also an opportunity to connect with Los Angeles' rich history. The railway stands as a testament to the city's enduring commitment to preserving its cultural heritage while continuing to evolve as a dynamic urban center.

Hollywood Walk of Fame

The Hollywood Walk of Fame is one of the most famous and recognizable landmarks in Los Angeles, attracting millions of visitors from around the world each year. Stretching along 15 blocks of Hollywood Boulevard and three blocks of Vine Street, this iconic sidewalk honors the achievements of those in the entertainment industry with over 2,600 brass stars embedded in pink terrazzo.

Established in 1960, the Walk of Fame was conceived as a way to maintain the glamour and allure of Hollywood during a time when the area was undergoing significant redevelopment. The Hollywood Chamber of Commerce spearheaded the project, aiming to celebrate the achievements of actors, musicians, directors, producers, and other entertainment professionals who have made significant contributions to the industry.

The stars on the Walk of Fame are divided into five categories: motion pictures, television, music, radio, and live performance. Each star features the name of the honoree and an emblem representing their category of contribution. Among the notable recipients are Marilyn Monroe, Elvis Presley, Walt Disney, and more contemporary figures like Denzel Washington and Jennifer Lopez.

The selection process for receiving a star is rigorous. Nominees are evaluated by the Walk of Fame Selection Committee, and honorees are required to attend a public unveiling ceremony, which has become a major media event. These ceremonies attract fans and press from all over the world, further enhancing Hollywood's reputation as the entertainment capital.

Beyond its role as a tribute to entertainment legends, the Hollywood Walk of Fame is a bustling tourist destination. Visitors flock to the area to find their favorite stars, take photographs, and explore nearby attractions such as the TCL Chinese Theatre, Madame Tussauds Hollywood, and the Hollywood Museum. Street performers and vendors add to the lively atmosphere, making a stroll along the Walk of Fame a unique and engaging experience.

The Hollywood Walk of Fame not only celebrates the achievements of the entertainment industry's finest but also serves as a vibrant symbol of Hollywood's enduring legacy. Its stars, embedded in the sidewalks of one of the world's most famous neighborhoods, continue to inspire and captivate generations of fans, preserving the magic and allure of Hollywood for years to come.

Museums and Cultural Attractions

The Getty Center

The Getty Center, located in the Brentwood neighborhood of Los Angeles, is a renowned cultural complex that offers an extraordinary blend of art, architecture, and breathtaking gardens. Opened in 1997 and designed by architect Richard Meier, the center is perched on a hilltop, providing stunning panoramic views of Los Angeles.

The Getty Center houses an extensive collection of European paintings, sculptures, and decorative arts, along with American and European photographs. Notable pieces include Vincent van Gogh's "Irises," Rembrandt's "Abduction of Europa," and works by artists such as Manet, Monet, and Cézanne. The museum also features temporary exhibitions that highlight diverse artistic traditions and contemporary works.

Architecturally, the Getty Center is a masterpiece. The complex is constructed from travertine stone, which gives it a distinctive and elegant appearance. The arrangement of the buildings around open plazas and the integration of natural light into the galleries enhance the visitor experience. The Central Garden, designed by artist Robert Irwin, is a highlight, featuring a maze of azaleas, a reflecting pool, and ever-changing horticultural displays.

The Getty Center is not just about its art and architecture; it is also a hub for scholarly research and conservation. The Getty Research Institute, located within the complex, provides resources and support for scholars in the humanities. The Getty Conservation Institute works on preserving cultural heritage worldwide, contributing to the preservation of important artworks and monuments.

Visitors access the Getty Center via a tram ride from the base of the hill, adding to the sense of entering a unique and serene cultural space. The center offers a range of educational programs, including lectures, workshops, and family activities, making it an engaging destination for visitors of all ages.

With its combination of world-class art, stunning architecture, and beautifully designed gardens, the Getty Center offers an enriching experience that attracts millions of visitors each year. It stands as a testament to the vision of J. Paul Getty and remains a vital cultural landmark in Los Angeles.

The Getty Villa

The Getty Villa, located in the Pacific Palisades neighborhood of Los Angeles, is a museum dedicated to the arts and cultures of ancient Greece, Rome, and Etruria. Opened in 1974, the villa was the original location of the Getty Museum and was designed to replicate the Villa dei Papiri, a Roman country house in Herculaneum.

The Getty Villa's collection includes over 44,000 antiquities, with objects dating from 6,500 BC to 400 AD. Highlights of the collection include Greek vases, Roman sculptures, and Etruscan artifacts. Notable pieces include the Lansdowne Heracles, a Roman marble statue, and the Statue of Victorious Youth, a rare Greek bronze. The villa also features rotating exhibitions that explore various aspects of ancient art and culture.

The architectural design of the Getty Villa is a significant attraction in itself. Modeled after the ancient Roman villa, it features classical architecture with columns, frescoes, and meticulously landscaped gardens. The gardens, inspired by ancient Roman horticultural designs, include peristyles, reflecting pools, and a herb garden with plants known to the ancients.

Educational programs at the Getty Villa are extensive, offering lectures, performances, and hands-on workshops that engage visitors with the ancient world. The villa's theater, an outdoor space modeled after ancient Greek and Roman theaters, hosts classical plays and concerts, providing a unique cultural experience.

The Getty Villa also serves as a center for conservation and research in ancient art. The villa's conservation laboratories work on the preservation and study of antiquities, contributing to the broader field of art conservation. The villa's library, which houses a comprehensive collection of books and journals on classical art and archaeology, is a valuable resource for scholars.

Visiting the Getty Villa is an immersive experience that transports visitors back to the classical world. Its stunning setting on a hill overlooking the Pacific Ocean adds to its allure, making it a must-visit destination for anyone interested in ancient art and culture. The Getty Villa's commitment to education, conservation, and public engagement ensures that it remains a vibrant and essential part of Los Angeles' cultural landscape.

Los Angeles County Museum of Art (LACMA)

The Los Angeles County Museum of Art (LACMA) is the largest art museum in the western United States, located on Museum Row along Wilshire Boulevard. Established in 1965, LACMA is renowned for its vast and diverse collection, which spans over 6,000 years of artistic expression from around the world.

LACMA's permanent collection includes over 150,000 works of art, ranging from ancient artifacts to contemporary masterpieces. The museum's holdings are particularly strong in areas such as American and Latin American art, Asian art, and Islamic art. Highlights of the collection include Diego Rivera's "Portrait of Frida Kahlo," Chris Burden's "Urban Light," and a significant array of modern and contemporary works by artists like Andy Warhol, Jasper Johns, and Barbara Kruger.

One of LACMA's most recognizable installations is Chris Burden's "Urban Light," a large-scale sculpture composed of 202 restored cast-iron street lamps. This installation has become an iconic symbol of the museum and a popular spot for visitors to take photos. Another highlight is Michael Heizer's "Levitated Mass," a massive granite boulder that appears to float above a walkway, creating a dramatic visual effect.

The museum's campus is currently undergoing a significant transformation, with the construction of the David Geffen Galleries set to open in the coming years. Designed by architect Peter Zumthor, the new building will provide state-of-the-art exhibition spaces and further enhance the visitor experience. This ambitious project reflects LACMA's commitment to innovation and its role as a leading cultural institution.

LACMA offers a wide range of educational programs and community outreach initiatives. These include lectures, workshops, and art-making activities that engage visitors of all ages. The museum's commitment to accessibility is evident in its free admission programs for children and the use of technology to enhance the visitor experience.

With its extensive collection, innovative exhibitions, and commitment to public engagement, LACMA offers an unparalleled experience for art enthusiasts. The museum's dynamic presence in Los Angeles continues to inspire and educate, making it a vital part of the city's cultural landscape.

Whether exploring ancient artifacts or contemporary installations, visitors to LACMA are sure to find something that captivates and challenges their imagination.

The Broad

The Broad, located in downtown Los Angeles, is a contemporary art museum that has become a cultural beacon since its opening in 2015. Founded by philanthropists Eli and Edythe Broad, the museum is renowned for its striking architecture and impressive collection of postwar and contemporary art. The building, designed by the architectural firm Diller Scofidio + Renfro, features a distinctive "veil-and-vault" design, characterized by its honeycomb-like exterior that allows natural light to permeate the interior galleries.

The Broad's collection includes over 2,000 works by some of the most significant artists of the 20th and 21st centuries. Highlights include pieces by Jeff Koons, Cindy Sherman, Jean-Michel Basquiat, and Yayoi Kusama. One of the most popular exhibits is Kusama's "Infinity Mirrored Room – The Souls of Millions of Light Years Away," an immersive installation that creates a mesmerizing, reflective environment.

The museum's layout is designed to provide a fluid and engaging visitor experience. The "vault," located on the lower level, houses the collection's storage and curatorial spaces, while the "veil" encompasses the public galleries on the upper floors. This innovative design allows visitors to gain insight into the behind-the-scenes operations of the museum and enhances their understanding of the art on display.

The Broad offers free general admission, which has helped attract a diverse audience and foster a greater appreciation for contemporary art. The museum also hosts temporary exhibitions, public programs, and events that explore various aspects of modern and contemporary art, providing a dynamic cultural experience.

The Broad's central location in downtown Los Angeles places it within walking distance of other notable cultural institutions, such as the Walt Disney Concert Hall and the Museum of Contemporary Art (MOCA). This proximity creates a vibrant cultural corridor that attracts art lovers from around the world.

With its cutting-edge architecture, world-class collection, and commitment to accessibility, The Broad has quickly become a must-visit destination for anyone interested in contemporary art. The museum's dynamic presence continues to enrich Los Angeles' cultural landscape and inspire visitors from all walks of life.

Natural History Museum of Los Angeles County

The Natural History Museum of Los Angeles County (NHMLA) is a treasure trove of natural and cultural history, located in Exposition Park. Opened in 1913, it is the largest natural and historical museum in the western United States, housing over 35 million specimens and artifacts. The museum's extensive collections and engaging exhibits provide an in-depth look at the natural world and human history.

One of the museum's most popular attractions is its Dinosaur Hall, which features more than 300 fossils and 20 complete skeletons of prehistoric creatures, including a fearsome Tyrannosaurus rex and a Triceratops. The interactive displays and life-sized models offer an immersive experience that captivates visitors of all ages.

The museum also boasts an impressive collection of gems and minerals, showcasing over 2,000 specimens from around the world. The Gem and Mineral Hall dazzles visitors with its stunning array of precious stones, crystals, and meteorites. Another highlight is the Age of Mammals exhibit, which traces the evolution of mammals over the past 65 million years through fossils, models, and interactive displays.

NHMLA's Nature Gardens and Nature Lab offer visitors a chance to explore the biodiversity of Southern California. The outdoor gardens are home to a variety of native plants and wildlife, providing a living extension of the museum's exhibits. The Nature Lab features hands-on activities and live animal displays that educate visitors about urban ecology and conservation.

The museum also delves into human history with exhibits like Becoming Los Angeles, which chronicles the region's transformation from a remote pueblo to a bustling metropolis. The museum's extensive cultural collections include artifacts from Native American, Latin American, and Pacific Islander cultures, offering insights into the diverse heritage of the region.

NHMLA is committed to education and community engagement, offering a range of programs for students, families, and educators. These include workshops, lectures, and special events that foster a deeper understanding of science and history.

With its vast collections, interactive exhibits, and educational programs, the Natural History Museum of Los Angeles County provides a fascinating journey through the natural and cultural history of our world. It remains a vital cultural institution, inspiring curiosity and learning in visitors of all ages.

California Science Center

The California Science Center, located in Exposition Park, is a dynamic and interactive museum that inspires curiosity and discovery through its engaging exhibits and educational programs. Opened in 1998, the center has become one of Los Angeles' most popular attractions, offering visitors a hands-on exploration of science, technology, and innovation.

One of the most iconic exhibits at the California Science Center is the Space Shuttle Endeavour, which completed 25 missions between 1992 and 2011. The Endeavour is displayed in the Samuel Oschin Pavilion, where visitors can get an up-close look at the shuttle and learn about its history and the science of space exploration. Plans are underway to house the shuttle in a new, permanent exhibit that will display it in a vertical, launch-ready position.

The center's Ecosystems exhibit is another major highlight, featuring an impressive array of live plants and animals in various environmental settings. Visitors can explore eight different zones, including a desert, a polar region, and a kelp forest, each showcasing the unique adaptations and interactions of living organisms within their habitats. The exhibit also includes a 188,000-gallon tank housing a diverse community of marine life.

The World of Life exhibit delves into the biological processes that sustain life, from the cellular level to entire ecosystems. Interactive displays and models help visitors understand concepts such as genetics, metabolism, and the human body's functions. The Creative World exhibit focuses on engineering and technology, exploring topics like transportation, energy, and structural design through hands-on activities and real-world applications.

The California Science Center also features an IMAX theater, where visitors can watch educational films on a seven-story screen. These films complement the center's exhibits, offering immersive experiences that transport viewers to the depths of the ocean, outer space, and other fascinating environments.

The center is dedicated to science education and outreach, offering a variety of programs for students, teachers, and families. These include field trips, summer camps, and professional development workshops that aim to foster a lifelong love of learning and discovery.

With its diverse exhibits, interactive experiences, and commitment to education, the California Science Center provides a stimulating environment for exploring the wonders of science and technology. It continues to be a vital resource for the community, inspiring future generations of scientists, engineers, and innovators.

Museum of Contemporary Art (MOCA)

The Museum of Contemporary Art (MOCA), located in downtown Los Angeles, is a leading institution dedicated to contemporary art. Established in 1979, MOCA is unique among American museums as it was founded by artists, and it remains one of the most important venues for contemporary art on the West Coast. MOCA operates three distinct venues: MOCA Grand Avenue, The Geffen Contemporary at MOCA, and MOCA Pacific Design Center.

MOCA's collection includes over 7,000 works of art created after 1940, featuring a diverse array of mediums such as painting, sculpture, photography, video, and installation art. The museum's holdings encompass key movements in contemporary art, including Abstract Expressionism, Minimalism, Pop Art, Conceptual Art, and Postmodernism. Artists represented in the collection include Jackson Pollock, Andy Warhol, Roy Lichtenstein, Barbara Kruger, and Jean-Michel Basquiat.

MOCA Grand Avenue, designed by architect Arata Isozaki, serves as the museum's primary exhibition space. It hosts rotating exhibitions that highlight both established and emerging artists. The Geffen Contemporary at MOCA, located in a former warehouse in Little Tokyo, offers a more industrial and flexible space for large-scale installations and experimental works. MOCA Pacific Design Center, situated in West Hollywood, focuses on design and architecture, presenting innovative and cutting-edge exhibitions.

In addition to its impressive collection and exhibitions, MOCA is committed to public engagement and education. The museum offers a wide range of programs, including artist talks, panel discussions, workshops, and family activities. These programs aim to foster a deeper understanding of contemporary art and its relevance to contemporary society.

MOCA also plays a vital role in the cultural landscape of Los Angeles by supporting local artists and contributing to the city's vibrant arts scene. The museum collaborates with other cultural institutions, artists, and communities to create dynamic and inclusive programming.

With its extensive collection, innovative exhibitions, and commitment to public education, MOCA provides an enriching experience for art enthusiasts and newcomers alike. It remains a crucial platform for contemporary art, reflecting the dynamic and ever-evolving nature of the artistic landscape.

Petersen Automotive Museum

The Petersen Automotive Museum, located on Museum Row along Wilshire Boulevard in Los Angeles, is one of the largest and most prestigious automotive museums in the world. Established in 1994 by magazine publisher Robert E. Petersen and his wife Margie, the museum underwent a significant renovation in 2015, transforming it into an architectural and cultural landmark with a striking, futuristic façade designed by Kohn Pedersen Fox Associates.

The Petersen Automotive Museum's collection boasts over 300 vehicles, ranging from rare vintage cars to cutting-edge modern supercars. The museum's exhibits are designed to appeal to car enthusiasts of all ages, showcasing the history, engineering, and artistry of the automobile. The collection is displayed across three main floors, each dedicated to a different aspect of automotive culture.

The first floor, known as the History Floor, takes visitors through the evolution of the automobile, featuring iconic vehicles that have shaped automotive history. Highlights include early 20th-century classics, such as the 1913 Mercer Raceabout and the 1925 Rolls-Royce Phantom I, as well as influential American muscle cars and European sports cars.

The second floor, called the Industry Floor, delves into the design and manufacturing processes behind the creation of automobiles. This floor features exhibits on car customization, alternative fuel technologies, and the future of automotive design. Interactive displays and hands-on activities engage visitors in the engineering and innovation that drive the automotive industry.

The third floor, known as the Artistry Floor, celebrates the automobile as a work of art. This floor features stunning displays of coach-built luxury cars, concept cars, and vehicles that have achieved cultural significance through film, television, and celebrity ownership. Notable exhibits include the Batmobile from the 1989 "Batman" film and the DeLorean from "Back to the Future."

The Petersen Automotive Museum also offers the Vault, a guided tour experience that provides access to an extensive collection of rare and exotic cars not on regular display. The Vault showcases some of the most significant and valuable vehicles in the world, offering a unique and exclusive experience for car enthusiasts.

With its comprehensive collection, engaging exhibits, and educational programs, the Petersen Automotive Museum offers a fascinating journey through the world of automobiles. It stands as a testament to the enduring impact of the automobile on society and culture.

La Brea Tar Pits and Museum

The La Brea Tar Pits and Museum, located in Hancock Park in Los Angeles, is a unique destination that offers a fascinating glimpse into the prehistoric past. The tar pits, formed from natural asphalt seeping to the surface, have been trapping and preserving animals for tens of thousands of years, making it one of the richest Ice Age fossil sites in the world.

The La Brea Tar Pits were first discovered in the early 20th century, and since then, over a million bones have been excavated, representing more than 600 species of animals and plants. The tar pits have yielded an incredible array of fossils, including those of mammoths, saber-toothed cats, dire wolves, and giant ground sloths. The ongoing excavation and research efforts provide valuable insights into the life and environment of the Los Angeles Basin during the last Ice Age.

The adjacent George C. Page Museum, commonly known as the La Brea Tar Pits Museum, houses an extensive collection of fossils recovered from the tar pits. The museum's exhibits showcase the rich biodiversity of the region during the Pleistocene epoch, with life-sized models, dioramas, and interactive displays that bring these ancient creatures to life. Visitors can view real fossils being prepared in the museum's glass-walled Fossil Lab, offering a behind-the-scenes look at the meticulous work of paleontologists.

One of the museum's most iconic displays is the reconstructed skeleton of a Columbian mammoth, which greets visitors at the entrance. Other notable exhibits include the Fossil Wall, featuring hundreds of fossilized bones, and the interactive Tar Pull, where visitors can experience the difficulty of pulling objects out of tar.

The outdoor areas of the La Brea Tar Pits and Museum are equally engaging, with active excavation sites known as Project 23, where visitors can observe paleontologists at work. The tar pits themselves, with their bubbling asphalt pools, provide a striking visual reminder of the area's ancient and ongoing geological activity.

Educational programs at the La Brea Tar Pits and Museum include guided tours, workshops, and lectures that cater to audiences of all ages. These programs aim to educate visitors about the significance of the tar pits and the scientific processes involved in uncovering and studying fossils.

With its unique combination of active research, engaging exhibits, and historical significance, the La Brea Tar Pits and Museum offers a captivating experience for visitors. It serves as a window into the prehistoric past and highlights the importance of paleontological research in understanding our planet's history.

The Grammy Museum

The Grammy Museum, located in the L.A. Live entertainment complex in downtown Los Angeles, is a dynamic and interactive museum dedicated to celebrating the history and impact of music. Opened in 2008, the museum offers visitors an in-depth look at the Grammy Awards, the music industry, and the artists who have shaped popular music across genres and generations.

The Grammy Museum's exhibits cover a wide range of musical styles, from rock and pop to jazz, classical, and hip-hop. The museum features an extensive collection of artifacts, including costumes, instruments, handwritten lyrics, and personal items from iconic musicians. Notable pieces include Michael Jackson's "Thriller" jacket, Ella Fitzgerald's Grammy Awards, and the guitar used by Johnny Cash.

One of the museum's highlights is the interactive exhibit space, where visitors can engage with music through hands-on experiences. The "Roland Live" exhibit allows visitors to play instruments and create their own music using professional-grade equipment. The "Crossroads" exhibit explores the intersections of different musical genres, highlighting how various styles have influenced one another over time.

The Grammy Museum also includes the "Clive Davis Theater," a state-of-the-art venue that hosts live performances, film screenings, and public programs. The theater provides an intimate setting for concerts and events, featuring both emerging artists and established musicians. The museum's public programs, including artist interviews, panel discussions, and educational workshops, offer unique insights into the music industry and the creative process.

The museum's temporary exhibits rotate regularly, ensuring there is always something new and exciting to explore. Past exhibits have focused on influential artists such as Bob Dylan, Whitney Houston, and The Beatles, as well as thematic exhibitions on topics like the history of hip-hop and the evolution of music technology.

Education is a core component of the Grammy Museum's mission, with programs designed to inspire and educate the next generation of musicians and music lovers. The museum offers a variety of educational initiatives, including school tours, workshops, and the Grammy Camp, which provides hands-on music industry experience for high school students.

With its comprehensive exhibits, interactive experiences, and commitment to music education, the Grammy Museum offers a vibrant and engaging exploration of the world of music. It stands as a testament to the power of music to inspire, connect, and transform, making it a must-visit destination for music enthusiasts and anyone interested in the cultural impact of the Grammy Awards and the music industry.

Parks and Outdoor Activities

Runyon Canyon Park

Runyon Canyon Park, located in the heart of Hollywood, is a popular urban park known for its scenic hiking trails, panoramic views, and vibrant social scene. Covering 160 acres, the park offers a natural escape within the bustling city, attracting fitness enthusiasts, nature lovers, and celebrities alike.

The park's main draw is its extensive network of trails, which cater to hikers of all skill levels. The primary routes include the Runyon Canyon Road, the East Trail, and the West Trail. These trails vary in difficulty, with the East Trail being the most challenging due to its steep inclines. Regardless of the chosen path, hikers are rewarded with stunning views of the Los Angeles skyline, the Hollywood Sign, and the Pacific Ocean.

Runyon Canyon's open and accessible environment makes it a favorite destination for dog owners. The park features designated off-leash areas where dogs can roam freely, socializing and exercising alongside their owners. This pet-friendly atmosphere adds to the park's lively and community-oriented vibe.

In addition to hiking and dog walking, Runyon Canyon offers several yoga classes that take advantage of the park's serene and picturesque settings. These outdoor classes provide a unique opportunity to practice yoga while immersed in nature, enhancing both physical and mental well-being.

The park's history is as rich as its natural beauty. The land was originally owned by Carman Runyon, a prominent figure in early Hollywood, who developed the area as a private estate before it was eventually donated to the city. Remnants of its past, such as the old estate gate and the remains of the Runyon mansion, add a touch of historical intrigue to the park.

Runyon Canyon Park's accessibility and diverse offerings make it a quintessential part of the Los Angeles outdoor experience. Whether visitors are looking to break a sweat on a challenging hike, enjoy a leisurely walk with their dog, or simply soak in the city's beauty from a high vantage point, Runyon Canyon provides an ideal setting for outdoor recreation and relaxation.

Santa Monica Mountains National Recreation Area

The Santa Monica Mountains National Recreation Area (SMMNRA) is a vast and diverse protected area that stretches across more than 150,000 acres from the Hollywood Hills to the Pacific Ocean. As the world's largest urban national park, it offers a unique blend of natural beauty, recreational opportunities, and cultural heritage within close proximity to Los Angeles.

The SMMNRA is renowned for its stunning landscapes, which include rugged mountains, rolling hills, and pristine beaches. The park's varied ecosystems support a rich array of flora and fauna, making it a haven for wildlife enthusiasts and nature lovers. Visitors can encounter species such as mountain lions, bobcats, and over 450 types of birds within its boundaries.

Hiking is one of the most popular activities in the SMMNRA, with over 500 miles of trails winding through its scenic terrain. Trails like the Backbone Trail, which spans nearly 70 miles from Point Mugu State Park to Will Rogers State Historic Park, offer hikers challenging and rewarding routes with breathtaking views of the mountains and coastline. The park also features easier trails suitable for families and casual hikers, such as the Solstice Canyon Trail, which leads to a picturesque waterfall and the ruins of a historic homestead.

The SMMNRA's coastal areas, including Zuma Beach and Malibu Lagoon, provide opportunities for swimming, surfing, and sunbathing. These beaches are famous for their natural beauty and relatively unspoiled conditions, attracting both locals and tourists seeking a peaceful retreat by the sea.

In addition to its natural attractions, the SMMNRA is rich in cultural history. The park contains numerous archaeological sites, including Native American rock art and remnants of early Spanish settlements. Historic ranches and estates, such as the Paramount Ranch and King Gillette Ranch, offer a glimpse into the region's past and serve as popular locations for filming and events.

The Santa Monica Mountains National Recreation Area also plays a vital role in environmental education and conservation. The park hosts a variety of programs, including ranger-led hikes, wildlife observation sessions, and educational workshops that promote awareness and appreciation of the natural world.

With its diverse landscapes, abundant recreational opportunities, and rich cultural heritage, the Santa Monica Mountains National Recreation Area offers a unique and immersive experience for visitors. It stands as a testament to the natural beauty and ecological significance of the region, providing a cherished escape for those seeking to explore and enjoy the great outdoors.

Echo Park Lake

Echo Park Lake, nestled in the heart of Los Angeles, is a beloved urban oasis offering a tranquil retreat from the bustling city. Originally constructed in the 1860s as a reservoir, the lake and its surrounding park have become a focal point for community recreation and cultural events. The park underwent significant renovations in 2013, revitalizing its landscape and infrastructure to better serve the public.

The centerpiece of Echo Park Lake is its picturesque lake, adorned with blooming lotus flowers and dotted with pedal boats available for rent. Visitors can enjoy a leisurely paddle across the serene waters, offering a unique perspective of the city skyline. The lake is also home to a variety of bird species, making it a popular spot for birdwatching and nature photography.

Surrounding the lake is a well-maintained walking path that invites joggers, walkers, and cyclists to explore the scenic environment. Benches and picnic areas provide ideal spots for relaxation, socializing, and enjoying the outdoors. The park's lush greenery and colorful flower beds enhance its appeal, creating a serene environment for visitors.

Echo Park Lake is also known for its iconic Lady of the Lake statue, a historic landmark that adds to the park's charm. The statue, along with the park's boathouse and other historic structures, reflects the rich cultural heritage of the area. The park frequently hosts community events, including outdoor concerts, art festivals, and farmers' markets, fostering a sense of community and engagement.

One of the highlights of Echo Park Lake is its annual Lotus Festival, celebrating the blooming of the lake's lotus flowers. This vibrant event features cultural performances, food vendors, and family-friendly activities, drawing crowds from across the city. The festival honors the diverse Asian and Pacific Islander communities in Los Angeles, showcasing their cultural traditions and contributions.

Echo Park Lake's combination of natural beauty, recreational opportunities, and cultural significance makes it a cherished destination for residents and visitors alike. Whether enjoying a peaceful boat ride, a scenic stroll, or a lively community event, visitors to Echo Park Lake are sure to find a welcoming and enriching experience.

Exposition Park

Exposition Park, located in the heart of Los Angeles, is a sprawling urban park that encompasses a variety of cultural, educational, and recreational attractions. Established in 1872, the park has evolved into a vibrant destination, attracting millions of visitors each year with its diverse offerings and rich history.

One of the park's most notable attractions is the California Science Center, a state-of-the-art facility that inspires curiosity and learning through its interactive exhibits and educational programs. The center's highlight is the Space Shuttle Endeavour, displayed in the Samuel Oschin Pavilion. Visitors can get an up-close look at this iconic spacecraft and explore the science and technology behind space exploration.

Adjacent to the California Science Center is the Natural History Museum of Los Angeles County, which houses an extensive collection of artifacts and specimens. The museum's Dinosaur Hall, featuring life-sized dinosaur skeletons and interactive displays, is a favorite among visitors. The museum also offers exhibits on ancient cultures, gemstones, and the natural history of Southern California.

Exposition Park is also home to the Los Angeles Memorial Coliseum, a historic sports venue that has hosted two Olympic Games and numerous other significant events. The Coliseum remains an active stadium, serving as the home field for USC Trojans football and hosting various concerts and public events.

The park's lush grounds include the Exposition Park Rose Garden, a beautiful and tranquil area featuring thousands of blooming roses. Established in 1928, the garden is a popular spot for weddings, picnics, and leisurely strolls. Its well-maintained pathways and colorful flower beds create a picturesque setting that offers a peaceful retreat within the bustling city.

The California African American Museum (CAAM), also located within Exposition Park, showcases the history, art, and culture of African

Americans, with a focus on California and the western United States. The museum's dynamic exhibitions and public programs celebrate the contributions and achievements of African Americans, fostering greater understanding and appreciation.

With its rich blend of cultural institutions, recreational spaces, and historical landmarks, Exposition Park offers something for everyone. It serves as a vital cultural hub in Los Angeles, providing educational and recreational opportunities that enrich the lives of residents and visitors alike.

Malibu Beaches (Zuma Beach, El Matador State Beach)

Malibu, renowned for its stunning coastline and luxurious lifestyle, boasts some of the most beautiful beaches in Southern California. Among these, Zuma Beach and El Matador State Beach stand out as premier destinations for both locals and visitors seeking sun, surf, and natural beauty.

Zuma Beach, one of the largest and most popular beaches in Malibu, offers expansive stretches of golden sand and clear, inviting waters. It is well-known for its excellent facilities, including ample parking, restrooms, showers, and lifeguard stations, ensuring a safe and comfortable experience for beachgoers. Zuma Beach is a haven for swimmers, surfers, and sunbathers, with its consistent waves and pristine shoreline. The beach is also a great spot for beach volleyball, picnicking, and long, scenic walks along the coast.

El Matador State Beach, part of the Robert H. Meyer Memorial State Beach, is famed for its dramatic landscape and secluded coves. This beach is characterized by its rugged cliffs, sea caves, and large rock formations that create a breathtakingly picturesque environment. Access to El Matador involves a short hike down a steep path and staircase, but the effort is rewarded with stunning views and a more intimate beach experience. Photographers and nature lovers are particularly drawn to El Matador for its scenic beauty, especially during sunset when the light casts a magical glow over the rocks and waves.

Both Zuma Beach and El Matador State Beach offer unique experiences that showcase the natural splendor of Malibu. Zuma Beach's wide, open spaces and family-friendly amenities make it ideal for a day of fun and relaxation, while El Matador's secluded and scenic spots provide a perfect escape for those seeking tranquility and a connection with nature.

Beyond their individual charms, these beaches are part of Malibu's larger coastal allure, which includes numerous other beaches, hiking trails, and scenic overlooks. Whether exploring tide pools, enjoying a picnic, or simply soaking up the sun, visitors to Malibu's beaches are sure to find a slice of paradise along this iconic stretch of the California coast.

Venice Beach Boardwalk

Venice Beach Boardwalk, an iconic and vibrant stretch along the Pacific Ocean in Los Angeles, is a bustling hub of activity and creativity. Known for its eclectic mix of street performers, artists, vendors, and unique characters, the boardwalk offers an unparalleled cultural experience that reflects the diverse and free-spirited nature of Venice Beach.

Stretching approximately two miles, the boardwalk is lined with an array of shops, cafes, and eateries, offering everything from souvenirs and local crafts to gourmet meals and quick snacks. The eclectic mix of street vendors adds to the boardwalk's lively atmosphere, with artists showcasing their work, musicians playing live music, and performers entertaining crowds with their talents.

One of the key attractions along the Venice Beach Boardwalk is Muscle Beach, an iconic outdoor gym where bodybuilders and fitness enthusiasts work out in the open air. This historic site has been a gathering place for fitness culture since the 1930s and continues to draw athletes and spectators alike. The nearby skate park, with its impressive ramps and bowls, is another popular spot, attracting skateboarders of all ages and skill levels.

The boardwalk also features numerous street art and murals that contribute to the area's vibrant aesthetic. These colorful and often thought-provoking artworks reflect the creativity and diversity of the local community. Visitors can take guided tours to learn more about the history and significance of these public art installations.

In addition to its cultural offerings, the Venice Beach Boardwalk provides access to the beach itself, where visitors can enjoy sunbathing, swimming, and beach sports. The wide, sandy shores and gentle waves make it a popular destination for both relaxation and recreation. The bike path running parallel to the boardwalk offers a scenic route for cyclists, rollerbladers, and joggers, stretching from Santa Monica to Marina del Rey.

Venice Beach Boardwalk's unique blend of artistry, entertainment, and beachside charm makes it a must-visit destination for anyone exploring Los Angeles. Its lively atmosphere and diverse attractions ensure that there is something for everyone, whether you're looking to shop, dine, people-watch, or simply soak in the bohemian vibe of this iconic locale.

Los Angeles Arboretum and Botanic Garden

The Los Angeles County Arboretum and Botanic Garden, located in Arcadia, California, spans over 127 acres of lush landscapes and diverse plant collections. Established in 1947, this historic garden is a haven for nature enthusiasts, horticulturists, and families seeking a serene escape from the urban bustle.

The Arboretum is renowned for its wide variety of themed gardens and plant collections that showcase flora from around the world. Visitors can explore the Tropical Greenhouse, filled with exotic plants and orchids, or wander through the Australian Garden, featuring native plants like eucalyptus and acacia. The Rose Garden, with its vibrant blooms, offers a fragrant and picturesque setting, while the Meadowbrook Garden provides a tranquil space with flowing streams and shady trees.

One of the Arboretum's most iconic features is the Queen Anne Cottage, a Victorian-era building surrounded by picturesque landscapes and often recognized from its appearances in film and television. Nearby, the Baldwin Lake provides a habitat for various waterfowl and aquatic plants, adding to the garden's ecological diversity.

The Arboretum is not only a place of beauty but also a center for education and conservation. It offers numerous programs and workshops for adults and children, covering topics such as gardening, botany, and sustainability. The garden's educational efforts aim to promote awareness and appreciation of plant diversity and conservation.

In addition to its gardens and educational programs, the Arboretum hosts seasonal events that draw visitors year-round. The annual "Moonlight Forest" lantern art festival transforms the garden into a magical display of illuminated art, while the springtime "Garden Festival" celebrates the beauty of the season with plant sales, expert talks, and family-friendly activities.

The Los Angeles County Arboretum and Botanic Garden's combination of natural beauty, historical significance, and educational initiatives make it a cherished destination. Whether strolling through its diverse gardens, participating in a workshop, or enjoying a seasonal event, visitors to the Arboretum are sure to find inspiration and tranquility in this verdant retreat.

Descanso Gardens

Descanso Gardens, located in La Cañada Flintridge, California, is a stunning 150-acre botanical garden known for its diverse plant collections, serene landscapes, and rich history. Originally a private estate, Descanso Gardens was transformed into a public garden in 1953 and has since become a beloved destination for nature lovers and horticultural enthusiasts.

One of Descanso Gardens' most renowned features is its impressive collection of camellias, which bloom in vibrant shades of pink, red, and white from late fall to early spring. This collection, one of the largest in North America, draws visitors from all over to witness the stunning floral display. The Rose Garden, with its over 1,600 rose bushes, offers another spectacular sight, particularly during the peak bloom season in spring and summer.

The Japanese Garden is a tranquil area within Descanso Gardens, featuring a koi-filled pond, arched bridges, and traditional Japanese landscaping elements. This serene space provides a peaceful retreat where visitors can relax and reflect. The Oak Woodland, home to hundreds of native California oaks, showcases the beauty and resilience of these majestic trees.

Descanso Gardens also hosts a variety of seasonal events and activities that enhance the visitor experience. The annual "Enchanted: Forest of Light" event transforms the garden into a magical nighttime landscape with interactive light displays. The "Cherry Blossom Festival" celebrates the arrival of spring with cultural performances, activities, and the stunning blooms of cherry trees.

In addition to its beautiful gardens, Descanso Gardens offers educational programs and workshops for all ages. These programs cover a wide range of topics, including gardening, environmental conservation, and botanical art. The garden's mission to promote horticultural education and appreciation is evident in its community outreach and involvement.

The historic Boddy House, the former residence of the estate's original owner, E. Manchester Boddy, is another highlight of Descanso Gardens. Visitors can tour this elegant mansion and learn about the garden's history and the Boddy family's contributions to its development.

Descanso Gardens' combination of horticultural excellence, historical significance, and educational initiatives makes it a cherished destination. Whether exploring its diverse plant collections, participating in a workshop, or attending a seasonal event, visitors to Descanso Gardens are sure to find inspiration and tranquility in this botanical haven.

Palisades Park

Palisades Park, located in Santa Monica, California, is a scenic 26.4-acre park that stretches along the bluffs overlooking the Pacific Ocean. With its breathtaking views, lush landscapes, and vibrant atmosphere, Palisades Park offers a serene retreat for both locals and visitors seeking relaxation and natural beauty.

One of the most striking features of Palisades Park is its stunning ocean vistas. The park's elevated position provides panoramic views of the coastline, from Malibu to Palos Verdes, making it a popular spot for photography, picnics, and simply enjoying the sunset. The park's palm-lined pathways and well-maintained gardens add to its charm, creating a picturesque setting for leisurely strolls and outdoor activities.

Palisades Park is also home to a variety of plant species, including towering palm trees, colorful flower beds, and native Californian flora. The park's diverse plantings create a lush and inviting environment, attracting birds and other wildlife, making it a delightful spot for nature enthusiasts and birdwatchers.

The park features several notable landmarks and attractions that add to its appeal. The historic Camera Obscura, a unique optical device that offers a fascinating view of the surrounding area, is housed in a small building within the park. The "Singing Beach Chairs" art installation, a series of interactive sculptures that play musical notes when touched, provides a whimsical and engaging experience for visitors.

In addition to its natural beauty and landmarks, Palisades Park offers a range of recreational opportunities. The park's walking and jogging paths are popular with fitness enthusiasts, while the numerous benches and picnic areas provide comfortable spots for relaxation and socializing. The park's open grassy areas are perfect for yoga, meditation, and other outdoor activities.

Palisades Park also serves as a venue for community events and gatherings, enhancing its role as a vibrant public space. The park hosts seasonal celebrations, cultural festivals, and outdoor performances, bringing together people from all walks of life to enjoy the scenic surroundings and lively atmosphere.

With its breathtaking views, lush landscapes, and diverse recreational offerings, Palisades Park is a cherished destination in Santa Monica. Whether taking a peaceful stroll, enjoying a picnic, or participating in a community event, visitors to Palisades Park are sure to find a welcoming and inspiring environment that captures the essence of coastal California.

Kenneth Hahn State Recreation Area

Kenneth Hahn State Recreation Area is a hidden gem in the heart of Los Angeles, offering a vast expanse of green space and a variety of outdoor activities. Spanning over 400 acres, this urban park provides a serene retreat from the hustle and bustle of city life, making it an ideal destination for nature lovers, families, and outdoor enthusiasts.

Located in the Baldwin Hills, Kenneth Hahn State Recreation Area boasts a diverse landscape that includes rolling hills, open meadows, and lush forests. The park features several miles of hiking and biking trails, which offer stunning views of the Los Angeles skyline, the Pacific Ocean, and the surrounding mountains. These trails cater to all levels of hikers, from easy, flat paths to more challenging routes that ascend the hills.

The park is also home to several picturesque picnic areas, complete with tables, barbecues, and shade trees, making it a perfect spot for family gatherings and outdoor meals. The Japanese Garden, with its tranquil pond, bridges, and beautifully manicured plants, offers a peaceful escape within the park, providing a lovely setting for relaxation and contemplation.

Kenneth Hahn State Recreation Area is equipped with a range of recreational facilities, including playgrounds, a fishing lake, and sports fields. The park's fishing lake is stocked with trout and catfish, offering a popular spot for anglers of all ages. The sports fields and courts accommodate a variety of activities, including soccer, baseball, and basketball, providing ample opportunities for organized sports and casual play.

In addition to its recreational offerings, the park is a haven for wildlife, with numerous bird species, small mammals, and native plants thriving in its diverse habitats. Birdwatchers and nature enthusiasts will find plenty to explore and observe, especially in the park's wetland areas and along its streams.

Kenneth Hahn State Recreation Area also holds cultural and community events throughout the year, including outdoor concerts, fitness classes, and environmental education programs. These events foster a sense of community and encourage visitors to engage with nature and each other.

Overall, Kenneth Hahn State Recreation Area is a versatile and vibrant park that provides a wide array of activities and natural beauty. Its expansive green spaces, recreational facilities, and scenic trails make it a must-visit destination for anyone looking to experience the great outdoors in Los Angeles.

Entertainment and Nightlife

Hollywood Nightclubs and Bars

Hollywood is synonymous with glitz, glamour, and entertainment, making it a premier destination for nightlife enthusiasts. The area is dotted with an array of nightclubs and bars that cater to diverse tastes and preferences, ensuring an unforgettable night out in the heart of the entertainment capital.

Hollywood's nightclubs are legendary, offering everything from high-energy dance floors to exclusive VIP experiences. One of the most iconic venues is Avalon Hollywood, a historic club that has hosted legendary performances since the 1920s. Today, it is known for its state-of-the-art sound system, spectacular light shows, and top-tier DJs who spin a mix of electronic dance music that keeps the crowd moving all night long.

Another staple of Hollywood nightlife is Playhouse Hollywood, a hotspot for celebrities and partygoers alike. Known for its opulent décor and lively atmosphere, Playhouse features world-class DJs, elaborate theme parties, and a dance floor that pulses with energy. For those seeking an upscale experience, Warwick offers a chic and sophisticated setting with handcrafted cocktails, plush seating, and a stylish crowd.

Hollywood's bar scene is equally vibrant, offering a variety of settings for a more relaxed evening. The Roosevelt Hotel's historic bar, The Spare Room, combines classic cocktails with a vintage bowling alley, providing a unique and nostalgic experience. Good Times at Davey Wayne's, a 1970s-themed bar, is renowned for its retro ambiance, complete with a hidden entrance through a vintage refrigerator and a lively backyard patio.

For craft cocktail enthusiasts, No Vacancy offers an immersive experience in a historic Hollywood home, with expertly crafted drinks and secret performances. The rooftop bar at Mama Shelter provides panoramic views of the city skyline, along with a laid-back atmosphere perfect for enjoying drinks under the stars.

Hollywood's nightclubs and bars not only provide top-tier entertainment but also serve as cultural landmarks that capture the spirit and allure of Los Angeles nightlife. Whether dancing the night away at a high-energy club or sipping cocktails in a stylish bar, visitors are guaranteed a memorable night in Hollywood.

Downtown LA Nightlife

Downtown Los Angeles (DTLA) has experienced a dramatic transformation over the past decade, evolving into a vibrant nightlife destination that offers a mix of trendy bars, stylish clubs, and unique entertainment venues. The area's revitalization has brought a renewed energy, making it a hotspot for locals and tourists seeking diverse and dynamic evening experiences.

One of the highlights of DTLA nightlife is its rooftop bars, which provide stunning views of the city skyline along with creative cocktails and a chic ambiance. Perch, a French-inspired rooftop bistro, offers a cozy yet elegant atmosphere with fire pits, live music, and panoramic views that make it an ideal spot for a romantic evening or a night out with friends. Another popular venue is The Rooftop at The Standard, which features a pool, vibrant décor, and a lively crowd, making it a favorite for weekend gatherings and sunset drinks.

DTLA is also home to a variety of speakeasies and hidden bars that add an element of mystery and excitement to the nightlife scene. The Varnish, located behind a hidden door in Cole's French Dip, is renowned for its expertly crafted cocktails and intimate setting. Another gem is The Edison, housed in a historic power plant, which combines industrial chic décor with classic cocktails and live entertainment, including jazz bands and burlesque shows.

For those looking to dance the night away, Exchange LA is one of the premier nightclubs in the area. Set in the historic Los Angeles Stock Exchange building, this multi-level club features top DJs, cutting-edge lighting, and a high-energy atmosphere that attracts a fashionable crowd. Another standout venue is The Belasco, which offers a blend of modern and vintage elements with multiple dance floors, a rooftop lounge, and a diverse lineup of music events.

DTLA's cultural scene also contributes to its vibrant nightlife, with numerous theaters, galleries, and performance spaces hosting evening events. The Music Center and Walt Disney Concert Hall offer world-class performances ranging from classical music to contemporary dance, while the Ace Hotel's theater provides a historic setting for concerts, film screenings, and comedy shows.

With its eclectic mix of rooftop bars, hidden speakeasies, bustling nightclubs, and cultural venues, Downtown LA's nightlife offers something for everyone. Whether seeking an upscale night out, a casual evening with friends, or an immersive cultural experience, DTLA is the place to be after dark.

Live Music Venues

Los Angeles is renowned for its live music scene, and three of its most iconic venues—The Roxy, The Troubadour, and The Viper Room—stand out as essential destinations for music lovers. These historic clubs have hosted legendary performances and continue to be vibrant spots for discovering new talent and enjoying live music.

The Roxy Theatre, located on the Sunset Strip in West Hollywood, has been a cornerstone of the LA music scene since its opening in 1973. Known for its intimate setting and excellent acoustics, The Roxy has hosted an impressive array of artists across genres, from Bruce Springsteen and Bob Marley to contemporary acts like The Strokes and Lana Del Rey. The venue's storied history and ongoing commitment to live music make it a beloved spot for both performers and audiences.

The Troubadour, another iconic venue located in West Hollywood, opened its doors in 1957 and quickly became a launching pad for many famous musicians. This legendary club is known for its cozy, unpretentious atmosphere and its role in the careers of artists like Elton John, James Taylor, and Joni Mitchell. The Troubadour's dedication to showcasing emerging talent has cemented its reputation as a place where music history is made. With a capacity of around 500, the venue offers an up-close and personal concert experience that is cherished by fans and musicians alike.

The Viper Room, perhaps best known for its association with actor Johnny Depp, who co-owned the club in the 1990s, is another staple of the Sunset Strip. Since its opening in 1993, The Viper Room has cultivated a rock-and-roll edge, hosting performances by bands like Pearl Jam, The Strokes, and Queens of the Stone Age. The venue's dark, intimate setting and storied past create a unique atmosphere that continues to attract both established artists and up-and-coming bands.

Each of these venues offers a distinct experience, but they share a common thread: a dedication to live music and a rich history of unforgettable performances. Whether catching a rising star at The Troubadour, enjoying a legendary band at The Roxy, or experiencing the raw energy of The Viper Room, visitors are guaranteed a memorable night immersed in the vibrant LA music scene.

Comedy Clubs (The Comedy Store, Laugh Factory)

Los Angeles is a hub for comedy, and two of its most renowned comedy clubs—The Comedy Store and Laugh Factory—offer audiences the chance to see some of the best comedic talent in the world. These iconic venues have a storied history of hosting legendary performers and continue to be essential destinations for comedy lovers.

The Comedy Store, located on the Sunset Strip in West Hollywood, has been a cornerstone of the LA comedy scene since it opened in 1972. Founded by comedian Sammy Shore and his wife Mitzi, The Comedy Store quickly became a launchpad for some of the biggest names in comedy. Legends like Richard Pryor, Robin Williams, and Jim Carrey have all graced its stages. The club features three main rooms—the Original Room, the Main Room, and the Belly Room—each offering a unique atmosphere and a variety of shows. The Comedy Store is known for its open mic nights, where aspiring comedians can test their material, as well as its showcases that feature both established and up-and-coming comics.

Laugh Factory, located a short distance away on Sunset Boulevard, has been another staple of LA's comedy scene since it opened in 1979. Founded by Jamie Masada, the Laugh Factory is famous for its welcoming atmosphere and commitment to fostering comedic talent. The club has hosted performances by comedy giants such as George Carlin, Dave Chappelle, and Kevin Hart. The Laugh Factory is also known for its special events, including the annual Thanksgiving and Christmas charity shows where comedians perform for the homeless and underprivileged. With its emphasis on both legendary acts and fresh faces, the Laugh Factory provides a diverse and dynamic comedy experience.

Both The Comedy Store and Laugh Factory offer a quintessential Los Angeles experience, where audiences can enjoy top-tier comedy in intimate settings. Whether you're looking to see a favorite comedian or discover new talent, these clubs provide an evening of laughter and entertainment that reflects the vibrant spirit of LA's comedy scene.

Theaters and Performance Venues

Los Angeles is a city rich in cultural and theatrical experiences, and two of its premier theaters—Pantages Theatre and Ahmanson Theatre—stand out as must-visit destinations for anyone interested in live performance. These venues host a wide range of productions, from Broadway shows to contemporary plays, offering something for every theatergoer.

The Pantages Theatre, located in the heart of Hollywood, is a historic landmark that has been a fixture of LA's entertainment scene since it opened in 1930. Originally built as a movie palace, the Pantages boasts stunning Art Deco architecture, with lavish interiors that transport visitors to a bygone era of glamour and elegance. In the 1950s, the theater was the home of the Academy Awards, further cementing its place in Hollywood history. Today, the Pantages is best known for hosting major Broadway productions, such as "Hamilton," "The Lion King," and "Wicked." Its grand auditorium and state-of-the-art facilities provide an ideal setting for both large-scale musicals and intimate performances, making it a beloved venue for theater enthusiasts.

The Ahmanson Theatre, part of the Los Angeles Music Center in Downtown LA, offers a more modern but equally prestigious theater experience. Opened in 1967, the Ahmanson Theatre is known for its diverse programming, which includes everything from classic plays and musicals to innovative new works. The theater's flexible seating arrangement allows for various configurations, accommodating productions of all sizes and styles. Notable past performances include "The Phantom of the Opera," "The Book of Mormon," and "Dear Evan Hansen." The Ahmanson's commitment to artistic excellence and its role in bringing world-class theater to Los Angeles make it a cornerstone of the city's cultural landscape.

Both the Pantages and the Ahmanson Theatres provide unforgettable experiences for theater lovers. Whether attending a blockbuster musical at the opulent Pantages or a groundbreaking play at the contemporary Ahmanson, audiences are treated to high-quality productions in venues that celebrate the magic of live performance.

Casino Entertainment

Casino entertainment in Los Angeles offers a vibrant and thrilling nightlife experience, combining the excitement of gaming with top-notch dining, live entertainment, and luxurious amenities. While the city itself does not have casinos within its immediate boundaries due to California state laws, several prominent casino resorts are located just a short drive away, providing ample opportunities for a fun-filled getaway.

One of the most popular casino destinations near Los Angeles is , located in the city of Commerce. Known as the world's largest poker casino, Commerce Casino offers a vast array of poker games, including Texas Hold'em, Seven-Card Stud, and Omaha. The casino also features other table games such as blackjack, baccarat, and Pai Gow poker. In addition to gaming, Commerce Casino boasts several dining options, from casual fare to fine dining, as well as a luxurious hotel with amenities such as a spa and pool. Regular poker tournaments and special events attract both amateur and professional players, creating a dynamic and competitive atmosphere.

Another major casino near Los Angeles is The Bicycle Hotel & Casino, commonly referred to as The Bike. Located in Bell Gardens, The Bike offers a wide range of gaming options, including poker, blackjack, and baccarat, along with a vibrant casino floor featuring various table games. The attached luxury hotel provides guests with modern accommodations, a fitness center, and a rooftop pool. The Bike also hosts numerous poker tournaments, including the prestigious World Series of Poker Circuit events, drawing top talent from around the world.

Pechanga Resort Casino, located in Temecula, offers a comprehensive resort experience with a large casino floor featuring slot machines, table games, and a dedicated poker room. Pechanga is known for its luxurious amenities, including a world-class spa, multiple dining options ranging from casual to fine dining, and an award-winning golf course. The resort also features a state-of-the-art theater that hosts concerts, comedy shows, and other live entertainment events.

These casino resorts near Los Angeles provide an exciting escape for those looking to enjoy gaming, fine dining, and live entertainment. With their luxurious accommodations and diverse offerings, they offer a complete entertainment experience that rivals some of the best casino destinations in the world.

The Magic Castle

The Magic Castle, located in Hollywood, is one of Los Angeles' most unique and enchanting venues. This private clubhouse for the Academy of Magical

Arts is housed in a stunning Victorian mansion that dates back to 1909. Since its establishment as the Magic Castle in 1963, it has become a renowned hub for magicians and magic enthusiasts from around the world.

The Magic Castle offers an intimate and immersive experience in the art of magic. Guests can explore various performance spaces within the castle, each offering different styles of magic shows. The Palace of Mystery, the Parlor of Prestidigitation, and the Close-Up Gallery are just a few of the venues where magicians perform their tricks and illusions. These performances range from grand illusions and stage magic to close-up magic that happens right before your eyes.

One of the most intriguing aspects of the Magic Castle is its exclusivity. Admission is typically reserved for members and their guests, though non-members can gain entry by securing a guest invitation from a member or through special events. This exclusivity adds to the allure and mystique of the venue.

The Magic Castle also boasts elegant dining options, including the Castle's main dining room, which serves gourmet cuisine in a refined setting. Guests often enjoy dinner before or after attending the various magic shows, making for a complete evening of entertainment.

Throughout its history, the Magic Castle has hosted some of the most famous magicians in the world, including David Copperfield, Penn & Teller, and Lance Burton. The club also serves as a training ground for aspiring magicians, offering lectures, workshops, and a supportive community of magic enthusiasts.

In addition to its performances and dining, the Magic Castle is known for its whimsical decor, secret doors, and hidden passageways, which add to the overall magical experience. The venue's dedication to preserving and promoting the art of magic ensures that every visit to the Magic Castle is a memorable and enchanting adventure.

The Echo

The Echo, located in the vibrant Echo Park neighborhood of Los Angeles, is a premier music venue known for its eclectic programming and intimate atmosphere. Since opening its doors in 2001, The Echo has become a beloved spot for both local music fans and visitors seeking to experience the city's dynamic live music scene.

The Echo is part of a larger complex that includes The Echoplex, a sister venue located directly below it. Together, these venues host an impressive range of performances that span various genres, including indie rock, punk, electronic, hip-hop, and more. This diversity in programming ensures that there's always something exciting happening at The Echo, catering to a wide array of musical tastes.

One of the key features of The Echo is its intimate setting. With a capacity of around 350 people, the venue offers a close-up and personal concert experience that allows audiences to connect with the performers. This cozy environment, combined with excellent acoustics and a lively crowd, creates a memorable atmosphere for live music.

The Echo is also known for its support of emerging artists. Many bands and musicians who have gone on to achieve significant success played some of their early shows at The Echo. The venue's commitment to showcasing new talent makes it a vital part of Los Angeles' music ecosystem, offering a platform for up-and-coming acts to reach new audiences.

In addition to live music, The Echo hosts a variety of other events, including dance parties, DJ sets, and themed nights. These events often draw diverse crowds and contribute to the venue's reputation as a cultural hotspot in Echo Park. The venue's laid-back vibe and welcoming atmosphere make it a favorite gathering place for music lovers and creatives.

The Echo's prime location in Echo Park means it is surrounded by a thriving community of bars, restaurants, and shops, making it an ideal destination for a night out. Whether you're looking to discover new music, see a favorite band in an intimate setting, or simply enjoy the energetic atmosphere, The Echo offers an unforgettable live music experience in the heart of Los Angeles.

The Mayan

The Mayan, located in downtown Los Angeles, is a historic theater and nightlife venue known for its stunning architecture and vibrant events. Originally opened in 1927 as a lavish movie palace, The Mayan has since been transformed into a versatile event space that hosts concerts, dance parties, and cultural performances.

The Mayan's architecture is one of its most distinctive features. Designed in the elaborate style of Mayan Revival, the venue boasts intricate carvings, ornate details, and a richly decorated interior that transports visitors to the ancient civilizations of Mesoamerica. The theater's grandeur and unique design make it a visually striking location for any event.

As a live music venue, The Mayan offers an exceptional setting for concerts and performances. The theater's large stage, advanced sound and lighting systems, and spacious dance floor make it an ideal venue for a wide range of musical acts. Over the years, The Mayan has hosted performances by renowned artists across genres, from rock and electronic music to Latin and world music.

In addition to concerts, The Mayan is famous for its dance nights, which draw large crowds eager to experience its dynamic nightlife scene. Regular events such as Club Mayan feature top DJs spinning a mix of dance, electronic, and Latin music, creating an energetic atmosphere where guests can dance the night away. The venue's multiple levels and VIP areas provide a variety of experiences, from intimate lounges to lively dance floors.

The Mayan is also a popular venue for special events, including film screenings, cultural festivals, and private parties. Its historic charm and versatile space make it a sought-after location for a variety of gatherings and celebrations. The venue's commitment to providing high-quality entertainment and memorable experiences has solidified its reputation as a premier destination in Los Angeles.

Located in the heart of downtown LA, The Mayan is easily accessible and surrounded by a vibrant urban landscape. Its combination of historic architecture, diverse programming, and lively atmosphere makes it a standout venue that continues to attract locals and visitors alike, offering a unique and unforgettable nightlife experience.

The Novo

The Novo, situated in the L.A. Live entertainment complex in downtown Los Angeles, is a state-of-the-art music venue known for its modern amenities and exceptional live performances. Since its opening in 2008, The Novo has established itself as a premier destination for concerts and special events, attracting a wide range of artists and audiences.

With a capacity of approximately 2,400, The Novo offers an intimate yet spacious setting that allows for a close connection between performers and fans. The venue's design emphasizes comfort and visibility, with tiered seating and a large general admission floor that ensures excellent sightlines from every angle. Advanced sound and lighting systems enhance the concert experience, delivering top-notch acoustics and immersive visual effects.

The Novo's programming is diverse, featuring performances by artists across various genres, including rock, hip-hop, pop, electronic, and more. The venue has hosted concerts by well-known acts such as Kendrick Lamar, The Weeknd, and Florence + The Machine, as well as emerging artists and international stars. This eclectic lineup ensures that there is always something exciting happening at The Novo, catering to a broad spectrum of musical tastes.

In addition to live music, The Novo is a versatile event space that hosts comedy shows, film screenings, award shows, and corporate events. Its location within the L.A. Live complex makes it a convenient and attractive option for event organizers, with easy access to nearby restaurants, bars, and hotels.

The Novo's commitment to providing a high-quality entertainment experience extends to its amenities, which include multiple bars, VIP areas, and premium seating options. These features, combined with the venue's modern design and cutting-edge technology, create a luxurious and enjoyable environment for all attendees.

The Novo's prime location in downtown Los Angeles places it at the center of the city's vibrant entertainment district. Visitors can easily explore the surrounding attractions, such as the Microsoft Theater, Staples Center, and the Grammy Museum, making The Novo a key part of any night out in L.A.

With its blend of modern amenities, diverse programming, and prime location, The Novo offers an exceptional live entertainment experience.

Family-Friendly Attractions

Los Angeles Zoo and Botanical Gardens

The Los Angeles Zoo and Botanical Gardens, located in Griffith Park, is a sprawling 133-acre facility that provides a fascinating and educational experience for visitors of all ages. Established in 1966, the zoo is home to over 1,400 animals representing more than 270 species, many of which are rare or endangered.

The zoo is divided into various themed areas that reflect the natural habitats of the animals. Notable exhibits include the Rainforest of the Americas, which showcases the diverse wildlife of Central and South American rainforests, and the Elephants of Asia exhibit, which features a spacious habitat for Asian elephants complete with a bathing pool, waterfall, and mud wallows. Another highlight is the LAIR (Living Amphibians, Invertebrates, and Reptiles), which houses a variety of reptiles, amphibians, and invertebrates in beautifully designed environments.

In addition to its animal exhibits, the Los Angeles Zoo is also known for its extensive botanical gardens. The gardens feature a wide variety of plants from around the world, with sections dedicated to specific regions and ecosystems. Visitors can explore the native California garden, the cactus and succulent garden, and the tropical rainforest garden, among others. The integration of botanical gardens and animal exhibits enhances the zoo's educational mission by demonstrating the interconnectedness of plants and animals in their natural habitats.

The zoo offers a range of educational programs and activities designed to engage and inspire visitors. These include daily animal feedings and presentations, behind-the-scenes tours, and interactive exhibits. The Zoo School program provides hands-on learning experiences for children, while the Zoo Camp offers fun and educational activities during school holidays.

Conservation is a key focus of the Los Angeles Zoo. The zoo participates in numerous breeding programs for endangered species and supports conservation efforts both locally and globally. The zoo's efforts to protect and preserve wildlife are highlighted through educational displays and special events.

With its diverse animal collection, beautiful botanical gardens, and commitment to education and conservation, the Los Angeles Zoo and Botanical Gardens offers a rich and rewarding experience for visitors. Whether exploring the exhibits, participating in educational programs, or simply enjoying the natural beauty of the gardens, visitors to the zoo are sure to leave with a greater appreciation for the natural world.

Aquarium of the Pacific

The Aquarium of the Pacific, located in Long Beach, California, is a world-class marine science and conservation facility that offers an immersive and educational experience for visitors. Opened in 1998, the aquarium is home to over 12,000 animals representing more than 500 species, showcasing the diverse and vibrant marine life of the Pacific Ocean.

The aquarium is divided into several main galleries that highlight different regions of the Pacific Ocean. The Southern California & Baja Gallery features species native to the local waters, such as sea otters, giant sea bass, and colorful garibaldi. The Northern Pacific Gallery explores the chilly waters of the North Pacific, with exhibits featuring sea jellies, puffins, and sea dragons. The Tropical Pacific Gallery showcases the vibrant coral reefs and tropical fish of the South Pacific, including sharks, rays, and sea turtles.

One of the aquarium's most popular attractions is the Shark Lagoon, where visitors can get up close and personal with a variety of shark species. Touch pools allow guests to gently touch and interact with these fascinating creatures, providing a hands-on learning experience. Another highlight is the Lorikeet Forest, an outdoor aviary where visitors can feed and interact with colorful lorikeets in a lush, tropical setting.

The Aquarium of the Pacific is dedicated to marine conservation and education. The facility offers a wide range of educational programs, including school field trips, summer camps, and hands-on workshops. The aquarium's exhibits are designed to engage visitors of all ages, with interactive displays, informative presentations, and live demonstrations that highlight the importance of ocean conservation and the impact of human activities on marine ecosystems.

In addition to its exhibits, the aquarium hosts a variety of special events throughout the year, including cultural festivals, guest lectures, and family-friendly activities. These events provide additional opportunities for visitors to learn about marine life and conservation efforts in an engaging and entertaining way.

With its impressive exhibits, interactive experiences, and commitment to education and conservation, the Aquarium of the Pacific offers a captivating and enriching experience for visitors. Whether exploring the diverse marine life of the Pacific Ocean, participating in educational programs, or attending a special event, guests are sure to leave with a deeper understanding and appreciation of the ocean and its inhabitants.

Kidspace Children's Museum

Kidspace Children's Museum, located in Pasadena, California, is a beloved destination for families and children, offering interactive exhibits and hands-on learning experiences designed to inspire curiosity and creativity. Since its opening in 1979, Kidspace has grown into a 3.5-acre campus featuring indoor and outdoor exhibits that cater to children of all ages.

The museum's exhibits are designed to engage children in playful learning across various disciplines, including science, art, and nature. One of the most popular exhibits is the Arroyo Adventure, an outdoor play area that encourages exploration and discovery through activities such as climbing, water play, and nature exploration. Children can dig for fossils, navigate a climbing wall, and splash in a stream, all while learning about the natural world.

Another highlight is the Imagination Workshop, where children can unleash their creativity through hands-on building and crafting projects. Equipped with tools, materials, and workstations, this exhibit encourages children to design, build, and experiment, fostering problem-solving skills and innovation. The Nature Exchange is another unique feature, allowing children to trade natural items they find and learn about the environment through hands-on exploration.

Kidspace also offers a variety of indoor exhibits that cater to younger children. The Early Childhood Learning Center provides a safe and stimulating environment for toddlers and preschoolers, with age-appropriate activities that promote cognitive and motor development. The Physics Forest is an outdoor exhibit area that features interactive displays demonstrating fundamental principles of physics, such as gravity, force, and motion, through fun and engaging activities.

In addition to its exhibits, Kidspace Children's Museum offers a wide range of educational programs and workshops. These include school field trips, summer camps, and family workshops that provide opportunities for hands-on learning and enrichment. Special events, such as seasonal festivals and themed days, add to the museum's appeal, offering unique and memorable experiences for visitors.

Kidspace is also committed to accessibility and inclusivity, providing resources and accommodations to ensure that all children can participate and benefit from the museum's offerings. With its focus on interactive learning and play, Kidspace Children's Museum provides a nurturing environment where children can explore, discover, and grow. Whether climbing, building, or experimenting, young visitors to Kidspace are sure to have a fun and educational experience that sparks their imagination and curiosity.

LEGOLAND California Resort

LEGOLAND California Resort, located in Carlsbad, is a premier family destination that brings the imaginative world of LEGO to life. Opened in 1999, this vibrant theme park offers a wide array of attractions, rides, and interactive experiences designed for children and LEGO enthusiasts of all ages.

The resort is divided into various themed areas, each offering unique attractions and experiences. Miniland USA, one of the park's highlights, features intricate LEGO models of iconic American landmarks and cities, including New York, Washington D.C., and San Francisco, all built with millions of LEGO bricks. The attention to detail in these miniature recreations is astounding, captivating both children and adults alike.

LEGOLAND offers a variety of rides and attractions tailored to different age groups. Younger children can enjoy gentle rides such as Fairy Tale Brook and the Safari Trek, while older kids and families can experience the thrill of roller coasters like the Dragon Coaster and the Technic Coaster. The park also features interactive attractions like the LEGO Ninjago Ride, where guests can test their ninja skills using hand-gesture technology to fight virtual enemies.

In addition to rides, LEGOLAND California includes several themed play areas, such as the Pirate Shores water play area and the LEGO Friends Heartlake City, where children can meet their favorite LEGO characters and participate in themed activities. The Imagination Zone offers creative play opportunities with LEGO bricks, encouraging kids to build and create their own masterpieces.

The resort also features the SEA LIFE Aquarium, which provides an educational and immersive experience with marine life exhibits, interactive touch pools, and a walk-through tunnel surrounded by sharks and other sea creatures. This aquarium adds an educational dimension to the park, making it both fun and informative.

For those looking to extend their visit, LEGOLAND California Resort offers themed accommodations at the LEGOLAND Hotel and LEGOLAND Castle Hotel, both of which feature imaginative décor, interactive play areas, and family-friendly amenities.

With its blend of thrilling rides, creative play areas, and detailed LEGO displays, LEGOLAND California Resort offers a magical experience for families and LEGO fans. It is a place where imagination knows no bounds, providing endless opportunities for fun, learning, and adventure.

Discovery Cube Los Angeles

Discovery Cube Los Angeles, located in the San Fernando Valley, is a hands-on science center dedicated to inspiring and educating children and families about science, technology, engineering, and mathematics (STEM). Opened in 2014, the center features a wide range of interactive exhibits and educational programs designed to spark curiosity and foster a love of learning.

One of the standout exhibits at Discovery Cube Los Angeles is the Science of Hockey, an engaging and immersive experience that explores the principles of physics, engineering, and biology through the lens of hockey. Visitors can test their slap shot speed, learn about the biomechanics of skating, and discover the technology behind hockey equipment.

Another popular exhibit is the Eco Challenge, which encourages visitors to think about sustainability and environmental responsibility. Through interactive displays and games, children learn about recycling, water conservation, and the impact of their choices on the planet. The Discovery Market, a part of the Eco Challenge, simulates a grocery store environment where kids can practice making eco-friendly decisions while shopping.

Discovery Cube Los Angeles also features the Planetary Research Station, where visitors can explore the wonders of space through interactive exhibits and multimedia presentations. This area includes a simulated mission control center, a space capsule, and hands-on activities that teach about the solar system, space exploration, and the science of astronomy.

The center offers a variety of educational programs, including field trips, summer camps, and workshops that align with California's science curriculum standards. These programs provide hands-on learning experiences that enhance classroom education and promote critical thinking skills. Additionally, Discovery Cube hosts special events and traveling exhibits that bring new and exciting content to the center throughout the year.

Discovery Cube Los Angeles is committed to accessibility and inclusivity, offering resources and accommodations to ensure that all visitors can fully participate in and enjoy the exhibits. The center's engaging and interactive approach to science education makes it a beloved destination for families, educators, and children.

With its focus on interactive learning and STEM education, Discovery Cube Los Angeles provides a dynamic and stimulating environment where children can explore, experiment, and discover the wonders of science. It is a place where learning is fun and curiosity is encouraged, making it an essential destination for young minds eager to explore the world around them.

Travel Town Museum

Travel Town Museum, located in Griffith Park, Los Angeles, is a charming and educational destination dedicated to the history of transportation. Established in 1952, this open-air museum offers visitors a chance to explore a fascinating collection of vintage trains, vehicles, and related artifacts, providing a glimpse into the evolution of transportation in Southern California.

The museum's primary focus is on railroad history, and it features an impressive array of locomotives, passenger cars, and freight cars from various eras. Visitors can walk through and around these historic trains, gaining an appreciation for the craftsmanship and engineering of early rail travel. Notable exhibits include a Southern Pacific steam locomotive, a Union Pacific caboose, and the Santa Fe Railway's business car.

One of the unique aspects of Travel Town Museum is its hands-on approach to learning. Children and families are encouraged to climb aboard several of the trains, explore the interiors, and imagine what it was like to travel by rail in the past. This interactive experience helps bring history to life and makes learning about transportation engaging and fun.

In addition to its train exhibits, Travel Town Museum showcases a collection of vintage automobiles, horse-drawn carriages, and other transportation artifacts. These exhibits highlight the diverse modes of transportation that have shaped Southern California's development over the years. The museum's collection of antique fire engines and early automobiles provides a fascinating look at the evolution of road travel and emergency services.

Travel Town Museum also offers educational programs and activities for children and families. These include guided tours, hands-on workshops, and special events that celebrate transportation history and heritage. The museum's picnic area and adjacent miniature train ride make it a popular spot for family outings and school field trips.

The museum's volunteer organization, the Travel Town Museum Foundation, plays a crucial role in preserving and restoring the exhibits. Through their efforts, many of the trains and vehicles have been meticulously maintained, ensuring that future generations can continue to enjoy and learn from them.

With its unique focus on transportation history, interactive exhibits, and family-friendly atmosphere, Travel Town Museum offers a delightful and educational experience for visitors of all ages. It provides a fascinating journey through time, showcasing the innovations and developments that have transformed the way we travel.

El Capitan Theatre

El Capitan Theatre, located on Hollywood Boulevard, is a historic and iconic venue that offers a unique blend of cinematic and live entertainment. Originally opened in 1926, the theater has undergone several transformations over the decades, ultimately becoming a premier destination for Disney movie premieres and special events.

The El Capitan Theatre's opulent interior is a stunning example of Spanish Colonial Revival architecture, with lavish decor that transports visitors back to the golden age of Hollywood. The theater's grand auditorium features intricate murals, a magnificent ceiling, and a classic Wurlitzer organ, which is often played before screenings, adding to the nostalgic ambiance.

One of the defining features of El Capitan Theatre is its close association with Disney. Since its acquisition by The Walt Disney Company in 1989, the theater has become the go-to venue for Disney film premieres and exclusive engagements. Audiences have the opportunity to be among the first to see new Disney, Pixar, Marvel, and Star Wars films in a setting that enhances the magic of the cinematic experience.

In addition to movie screenings, El Capitan Theatre offers a variety of special events and performances that make each visit memorable. These include live stage shows featuring Disney characters, interactive pre-show entertainment, and themed photo opportunities. The theater frequently hosts sing-along screenings, where audiences can join in on the fun by singing along to their favorite Disney songs.

El Capitan Theatre also provides unique behind-the-scenes tours, allowing visitors to explore the theater's rich history and architectural details. These tours offer insights into the theater's storied past, its connection to Hollywood's early days, and its transformation into a modern entertainment venue.

The theater's location on the iconic Hollywood Walk of Fame makes it an integral part of the Hollywood experience. Visitors can combine a trip to El Capitan with a stroll along the Walk of Fame, visits to nearby attractions like the TCL Chinese Theatre, and exploring the bustling Hollywood Boulevard.

With its historic charm, luxurious setting, and exclusive Disney programming, El Capitan Theatre offers a magical and immersive entertainment experience. Whether attending a film premiere, enjoying a live performance, or participating in a special event, guests at El Capitan are treated to a unique and unforgettable cinematic adventure in the heart of Hollywood.

Los Angeles Maritime Museum

The Los Angeles Maritime Museum, located in the bustling port of San Pedro, offers a rich exploration of the maritime history of Southern California. Housed in the historic Municipal Ferry Terminal building, which dates back to 1941, the museum provides an educational and engaging experience for visitors of all ages.

The museum's exhibits cover a wide range of maritime topics, including the history of the Port of Los Angeles, commercial shipping, naval operations, and recreational boating. One of the highlights is the collection of model ships, which showcases intricate replicas of various vessels, from early sailing ships to modern cargo carriers. These models provide a detailed look at the evolution of ship design and maritime technology.

Another significant exhibit is the display on the history of commercial diving, featuring vintage diving equipment and photographs that illustrate the development of underwater exploration and work. The museum also delves into the history of the U.S. Navy in the region, with exhibits highlighting the role of naval forces during World War II and the significance of the San Pedro harbor in military operations.

Visitors can explore the fully restored tugboat, the Angels Gate, which is docked just outside the museum. This hands-on exhibit allows guests to experience life aboard a working vessel and learn about the daily operations and challenges faced by maritime crews.

The museum's educational programs include guided tours, school field trips, and special events that bring maritime history to life. These programs are designed to engage students and visitors in learning about the maritime heritage of Los Angeles and the broader impacts of maritime trade and industry on the region.

With its rich collection of artifacts, detailed exhibits, and engaging educational programs, the Los Angeles Maritime Museum offers a comprehensive look at the maritime history that has shaped Southern California. Whether exploring the model ships, learning about commercial diving, or touring the historic tugboat, visitors are sure to gain a deeper appreciation for the region's nautical past.

Underwood Family Farms

Underwood Family Farms, located in Moorpark, California, is a beloved agricultural destination that offers a fun and educational experience for families and visitors of all ages. Spanning hundreds of acres, the farm provides a variety of activities that allow guests to connect with nature, learn about farming, and enjoy outdoor recreation.

One of the main attractions at Underwood Family Farms is the opportunity for visitors to pick their own produce. Depending on the season, guests can harvest a wide range of fruits and vegetables, including strawberries, blueberries, tomatoes, peppers, and pumpkins. This hands-on activity not only provides fresh, farm-to-table produce but also educates visitors about the different crops and the farming process.

The farm also features a large animal area where visitors can interact with a variety of farm animals, such as goats, sheep, chickens, rabbits, and ponies. Children especially enjoy feeding and petting the animals, making it a favorite activity for families. The farm also offers pony rides, tractor-drawn wagon rides, and a farm-themed playground, providing plenty of entertainment for younger visitors.

Throughout the year, Underwood Family Farms hosts several seasonal festivals and events that draw large crowds. The Fall Harvest Festival is particularly popular, featuring a pumpkin patch, corn maze, hay rides, and a variety of games and activities. Other events include the Springtime Easter Festival, which offers egg hunts and visits with the Easter Bunny, and the Christmas on the Farm event, which features holiday-themed activities and decorations.

Educational programs at Underwood Family Farms are designed to teach visitors about sustainable farming practices, the importance of agriculture, and the benefits of fresh produce. The farm offers school field trips, guided tours, and workshops that provide in-depth knowledge about farming and the environment.

With its combination of pick-your-own produce, animal interactions, seasonal events, and educational programs, Underwood Family Farms offers a unique and enjoyable experience for visitors. It is a place where families can spend quality time together, learn about agriculture, and enjoy the beauty of the natural world.

Sherman Oaks Castle Park

Sherman Oaks Castle Park, located in the heart of the San Fernando Valley, is a popular family entertainment center that offers a variety of fun activities for visitors of all ages. This medieval-themed amusement park features mini-golf, batting cages, arcade games, and more, making it a favorite destination for locals and tourists looking for a day of recreation and entertainment.

One of the main attractions at Sherman Oaks Castle Park is its beautifully designed miniature golf courses. The park boasts three 18-hole courses, each with its own unique challenges and whimsical decorations. The courses are set amidst lush landscaping, water features, and medieval-themed obstacles such as castles, drawbridges, and knights, creating a fun and engaging environment for players. Mini-golf at Castle Park is suitable for all skill levels, making it an enjoyable activity for families, friends, and groups.

In addition to mini-golf, Sherman Oaks Castle Park features state-of-the-art batting cages that cater to baseball and softball players of all ages and skill levels. The cages offer a range of pitching speeds, allowing visitors to practice their swings and improve their batting skills in a safe and controlled setting. The batting cages are a popular attraction for aspiring athletes and casual players alike.

The park's arcade is another major draw, offering a wide variety of classic and modern video games, redemption games, and prize machines. The arcade provides endless entertainment for children and adults, with games that test skills, reflexes, and strategy. Visitors can collect tickets from the games and redeem them for a variety of prizes, adding an extra layer of excitement to the experience.

Sherman Oaks Castle Park also hosts special events and offers party packages that make it an ideal venue for birthday celebrations, corporate events, and group outings. The park's event packages typically include access to the mini-golf courses, batting cages, and arcade, as well as food and beverages, ensuring a memorable and enjoyable experience for all attendees.

With its diverse range of activities, family-friendly atmosphere, and charming medieval theme, Sherman Oaks Castle Park provides a fun and engaging destination for a day out. Whether playing a round of mini-golf, practicing in the batting cages, or enjoying the arcade, visitors to Castle Park are sure to have a fantastic time filled with laughter and adventure.

Neighborhood Exploration

Hollywood

Hollywood, a neighborhood in Los Angeles, is synonymous with the glamour and allure of the entertainment industry. Known globally as the birthplace of American cinema, Hollywood offers a unique blend of history, culture, and modern attractions that draw millions of visitors each year.

One of the most iconic landmarks in Hollywood is the Hollywood Sign, perched atop the Hollywood Hills. This 45-foot-tall sign originally read "Hollywoodland" and was erected in 1923 as an advertisement for a real estate development. Today, it stands as a symbol of the entertainment industry and can be viewed from various points in the city, with Griffith Observatory offering particularly stunning views.

The Hollywood Walk of Fame is another major attraction, featuring over 2,600 stars embedded in the sidewalks along Hollywood Boulevard and Vine Street. These stars honor significant figures in the entertainment industry, from actors and musicians to directors and producers. Visitors often enjoy strolling the boulevard, finding their favorite stars, and taking photos with them.

Adjacent to the Walk of Fame is the TCL Chinese Theatre, renowned for its grand architecture and celebrity handprints and footprints in the forecourt. Since its opening in 1927, the theater has hosted countless movie premieres and special events, maintaining its status as a key venue in Hollywood's cinematic history.

Hollywood is also home to numerous museums and attractions dedicated to the film industry. The Hollywood Museum, located in the historic Max Factor Building, showcases memorabilia from classic films and television shows. The Dolby Theatre, home to the annual Academy Awards, offers guided tours that provide insights into the glitz and glamour of Hollywood's biggest night.

For those interested in contemporary entertainment, Hollywood offers a vibrant nightlife scene with trendy clubs, bars, and live music venues such as The Roxy, The Troubadour, and The Viper Room. The Hollywood Bowl, an iconic outdoor amphitheater, hosts concerts and performances by top artists and the Los Angeles Philharmonic.

With its rich history, iconic landmarks, and dynamic cultural scene, Hollywood remains a must-visit destination for anyone interested in the magic of the entertainment industry. It offers a fascinating glimpse into the past, present, and future of American cinema and popular culture.

Downtown LA

Downtown Los Angeles (DTLA) has undergone a remarkable transformation over the past two decades, evolving from a neglected urban area to a vibrant hub of culture, business, and nightlife. Today, DTLA is a dynamic destination that attracts locals and tourists with its diverse offerings, from historic landmarks to modern attractions.

One of the key highlights of Downtown LA is its rich architectural heritage. The historic core is home to many beautifully preserved buildings from the early 20th century, including the iconic Bradbury Building, known for its stunning ironwork and atrium. The nearby Los Angeles Central Library, an Art Deco masterpiece, offers a glimpse into the city's architectural past.

DTLA is also the cultural heart of Los Angeles, housing major institutions such as the Walt Disney Concert Hall, designed by renowned architect Frank Gehry. This striking building is home to the Los Angeles Philharmonic and offers world-class musical performances. The Music Center, which includes the Dorothy Chandler Pavilion, Ahmanson Theatre, and Mark Taper Forum, hosts a wide range of performances, from opera and ballet to theater and contemporary dance.

The Broad, a contemporary art museum, showcases an impressive collection of postwar and modern art, including works by artists like Jeff Koons, Cindy Sherman, and Jean-Michel Basquiat. Adjacent to The Broad is the Museum of Contemporary Art (MOCA), which also features cutting-edge exhibitions and installations.

For those interested in exploring DTLA's culinary scene, the area offers an array of dining options, from high-end restaurants to casual eateries. The Grand Central Market, a historic food hall, is a favorite spot for locals and visitors alike, offering diverse cuisine ranging from tacos and ramen to artisanal coffee and pastries.

Downtown LA's nightlife is equally vibrant, with trendy rooftop bars, historic speakeasies, and lively nightclubs. Venues like The Standard Hotel's rooftop bar provide stunning views of the city skyline, while The Edison, located in a historic power plant, offers a unique blend of vintage charm and modern cocktails.

With its mix of historic landmarks, cultural institutions, and modern attractions, Downtown LA offers a rich and diverse urban experience. Whether exploring its architectural gems, enjoying world-class performances, or sampling its culinary delights, visitors to DTLA are sure to find something that captivates and inspires.

Santa Monica

Santa Monica, located on the western edge of Los Angeles County, is a picturesque coastal city known for its beautiful beaches, vibrant pier, and laid-back atmosphere. With its stunning ocean views, lively downtown area, and numerous attractions, Santa Monica is a beloved destination for both locals and tourists seeking a quintessential Southern California experience.

One of the most iconic landmarks in Santa Monica is the Santa Monica Pier. This historic pier, built in 1909, features an array of attractions, including an amusement park, aquarium, and various dining and shopping options. Pacific Park, the pier's amusement park, is home to the famous Pacific Wheel, a solar-powered Ferris wheel that offers breathtaking views of the coastline. The pier is also a popular spot for fishing, leisurely strolls, and enjoying live entertainment.

Santa Monica Beach, stretching for 3.5 miles along the Pacific Ocean, is a major draw for sun-seekers and outdoor enthusiasts. The beach offers ample space for sunbathing, swimming, and beach sports, while the scenic Marvin Braude Bike Trail, also known as The Strand, runs along the shoreline and is perfect for cycling, jogging, and rollerblading.

Downtown Santa Monica is a bustling area filled with shops, restaurants, and entertainment options. The Third Street Promenade, a pedestrian-only shopping district, is lined with popular retail stores, cafes, and street performers, creating a lively and engaging atmosphere. Nearby, Santa Monica Place is an open-air shopping center offering a mix of high-end retailers and dining options.

For those interested in arts and culture, the Santa Monica Museum of Art and the Bergamot Station Arts Center provide opportunities to explore contemporary art and exhibitions. The city also hosts a variety of events and festivals throughout the year, including outdoor concerts, farmers' markets, and the annual Twilight Concert Series on the pier.

Santa Monica is also known for its commitment to sustainability and green living. The city has implemented numerous initiatives to promote environmental conservation, including extensive bike lanes, electric vehicle charging stations, and sustainable building practices.

With its blend of natural beauty, vibrant downtown area, and commitment to sustainability, Santa Monica offers a unique and enjoyable coastal experience. Whether relaxing on the beach, exploring the pier, or shopping and dining in the downtown area, visitors to Santa Monica are sure to enjoy its charm and relaxed vibe.

Venice Beach

Venice Beach, a vibrant and eclectic neighborhood in Los Angeles, is renowned for its bohemian spirit, artistic culture, and stunning beachfront. Established in 1905 by developer Abbot Kinney as a seaside resort town, Venice has since evolved into a dynamic and diverse community that attracts millions of visitors each year.

One of the most iconic features of Venice Beach is its boardwalk, also known as Ocean Front Walk. This bustling promenade stretches for about two miles along the Pacific Ocean and is lined with an array of shops, street vendors, and cafes. The boardwalk is a hub of activity, with street performers, musicians, and artists showcasing their talents, creating a lively and colorful atmosphere. Visitors can find everything from handmade crafts and jewelry to unique clothing and souvenirs.

Muscle Beach, an outdoor gym located on the boardwalk, is another major attraction. Known as the birthplace of the fitness boom in the 20th century, Muscle Beach has been frequented by famous bodybuilders like Arnold Schwarzenegger. Today, it remains a popular spot for fitness enthusiasts and spectators alike.

Venice Beach also boasts a beautiful and expansive shoreline, perfect for sunbathing, swimming, and beach sports. The beach's wide sandy areas and gentle waves make it ideal for surfing, volleyball, and other recreational activities. The Venice Beach Skate Park, located right on the sand, is a popular destination for skateboarders of all skill levels.

Beyond the beach and boardwalk, Venice is known for its unique architecture and canals. The Venice Canals, designed to mimic the canals of Venice, Italy, offer a picturesque setting with charming bridges, walkways, and historic homes. A stroll through the canals provides a tranquil escape from the bustling boardwalk.

Venice's Abbot Kinney Boulevard is a trendy shopping and dining destination, featuring a mix of high-end boutiques, artisanal shops, and gourmet restaurants. The street is also home to the monthly First Fridays event, where food trucks, live music, and art installations create a festive atmosphere.

With its blend of artistic culture, beachside activities, and eclectic charm, Venice Beach offers a unique and unforgettable experience. Whether exploring the boardwalk, enjoying the sun and surf, or discovering the local art scene, visitors to Venice Beach are sure to be captivated by its vibrant and dynamic spirit.

Beverly Hills

Beverly Hills, an iconic and affluent city in Los Angeles County, is synonymous with luxury, glamour, and celebrity culture. Known for its upscale shopping, exquisite dining, and opulent real estate, Beverly Hills attracts visitors from around the world who are eager to experience its unique blend of sophistication and charm.

One of the most famous landmarks in Beverly Hills is Rodeo Drive, a world-renowned shopping street that features a dazzling array of high-end boutiques, designer stores, and luxury brands. From Gucci and Prada to Chanel and Louis Vuitton, Rodeo Drive offers a shopping experience like no other, catering to those with discerning tastes and a love for fashion. The street's elegant storefronts, beautiful landscaping, and art installations add to its allure, making it a popular destination for tourists and locals alike.

In addition to its shopping, Beverly Hills is known for its luxurious hotels and fine dining establishments. The Beverly Hills Hotel, often referred to as the "Pink Palace," has been a favorite among Hollywood stars and international dignitaries since it opened in 1912. Another iconic hotel, the Beverly Wilshire, gained fame as the setting for the movie "Pretty

Woman." Both hotels offer world-class amenities, sumptuous dining, and a taste of old Hollywood glamour.

Beverly Hills also boasts a vibrant culinary scene, with a plethora of top-rated restaurants and cafes offering a wide range of cuisines. From Michelin-starred establishments to charming bistros, dining in Beverly Hills is a gastronomic delight that caters to every palate.

Beyond its shopping and dining, Beverly Hills is home to some of the most exclusive residential areas in the world. The tree-lined streets of neighborhoods like Beverly Hills Flats and Trousdale Estates are dotted with stunning mansions, lush gardens, and meticulously maintained properties. A drive through these neighborhoods offers a glimpse into the luxurious lifestyle of the city's affluent residents.

Beverly Hills also offers cultural and recreational attractions, including the historic Greystone Mansion, the Beverly Gardens Park with its famous Beverly Hills sign, and the scenic Mulholland Drive. The city hosts a variety of events throughout the year, such as the Beverly Hills Art Show and Concerts on Canon, providing entertainment and enrichment for residents and visitors alike.

With its combination of luxury, elegance, and cultural offerings, Beverly Hills remains an enduring symbol of the glamorous lifestyle that defines Southern California. Whether shopping on Rodeo Drive, dining at a five-star restaurant, or simply enjoying the picturesque surroundings, visitors to Beverly Hills are sure to be enchanted by its timeless appeal.

Silver Lake

Silver Lake, a trendy and diverse neighborhood in Los Angeles, is known for its artistic vibe, eclectic culture, and vibrant community. Situated just a few miles northwest of Downtown LA, Silver Lake has become a popular destination for young professionals, artists, and creatives seeking a lively and dynamic urban environment.

One of the defining features of Silver Lake is its namesake reservoir, which provides a scenic centerpiece for the neighborhood. The Silver Lake Reservoir is surrounded by a 2.2-mile walking and jogging path, as well as lush green spaces that offer a peaceful retreat from the hustle and bustle of city life. The nearby Silver Lake Meadow and Dog Park are popular spots for picnicking, relaxing, and enjoying outdoor activities.

Silver Lake is renowned for its unique and diverse architecture, with a mix of historic homes, modernist structures, and mid-century designs. The neighborhood is home to several notable examples of modernist architecture, including the iconic "Neutra VDL Studio and Residences," designed by renowned architect Richard Neutra. The winding streets and hillside locations provide stunning views of the city and create a distinctive and charming atmosphere.

The neighborhood's vibrant arts and culture scene is evident in its numerous galleries, studios, and creative spaces. Silver Lake hosts regular art walks, open studio events, and live performances that showcase the talents of local artists and musicians. The Silverlake Conservatory of Music, co-founded by Red Hot Chili Peppers' bassist Flea, offers music education and performances that contribute to the community's rich cultural fabric.

Silver Lake's dining and nightlife scene is equally eclectic, with a wide array of restaurants, cafes, bars, and coffee shops that reflect the neighborhood's diverse culinary influences. From artisanal bakeries and trendy brunch spots to gourmet food trucks and ethnic eateries, Silver Lake offers something for every palate. The neighborhood's nightlife is lively and varied, with cocktail bars, craft breweries, and live music venues providing ample entertainment options.

The neighborhood's independent boutiques and vintage stores add to its unique character, offering a curated selection of fashion, home goods, and accessories. The Sunset Junction area is a popular shopping destination, known for its stylish shops and hip atmosphere.

Silver Lake is also known for its community-oriented events and festivals, such as the Silver Lake Jubilee and the Sunset Junction Street Fair. These events bring residents and visitors together to celebrate the neighborhood's diverse culture and creative spirit.

With its blend of natural beauty, artistic energy, and vibrant community life, Silver Lake offers a distinctive and appealing experience. Whether exploring its scenic reservoir, enjoying its culinary delights, or immersing oneself in its cultural scene, visitors to Silver Lake are sure to be captivated by its unique charm and dynamic vibe.

Echo Park

Echo Park, located just northwest of downtown Los Angeles, is a vibrant and eclectic neighborhood known for its artistic spirit, diverse community, and picturesque lake. Established in the late 19th century, Echo Park has evolved into a cultural hotspot that attracts residents and visitors with its unique blend of history, nature, and contemporary urban life.

At the heart of the neighborhood is Echo Park Lake, a beautiful urban oasis that offers a tranquil retreat from the city's hustle and bustle. The lake, surrounded by walking paths and lush greenery, is a popular spot for picnicking, paddle boating, and birdwatching. The park's iconic lotus flowers bloom in the summer, creating a stunning natural display that draws crowds to the annual Lotus Festival, celebrating the area's Asian-American communities.

Echo Park's vibrant arts scene is evident in its numerous galleries, street art, and cultural events. The neighborhood is home to a diverse array of artists, musicians, and creatives who contribute to its dynamic atmosphere. The Echo and Echoplex, two renowned music venues, host an eclectic mix of live performances, from indie bands to established acts, making Echo Park a key destination for music lovers.

The neighborhood's diverse culinary scene reflects its multicultural population. Echo Park offers a wide range of dining options, from trendy cafes and vegan eateries to authentic Mexican, Thai, and Salvadoran restaurants. Sunset Boulevard, one of the main thoroughfares, is lined with hip coffee shops, boutique stores, and artisanal food markets, creating a lively and engaging environment.

Echo Park is also known for its historic architecture, with many well-preserved Victorian homes and Craftsman bungalows. The Angelino Heights area, in particular, features beautifully restored houses that provide a glimpse into Los Angeles' architectural past.

Community engagement is a hallmark of Echo Park, with numerous events and festivals fostering a strong sense of neighborhood pride. The Echo Park Farmers' Market, held weekly, offers fresh produce, local crafts, and live entertainment, bringing residents together in a vibrant community setting.

With its mix of natural beauty, artistic energy, and diverse cultural offerings, Echo Park offers a unique and enriching experience. Whether relaxing by the lake, exploring the local art scene, or enjoying its culinary delights, visitors to Echo Park are sure to be charmed by its eclectic and welcoming vibe.

Koreatown

Koreatown, commonly referred to as K-town, is a vibrant and densely populated neighborhood located just west of downtown Los Angeles. Known for its rich cultural heritage, bustling nightlife, and diverse culinary scene, Koreatown offers a unique blend of tradition and modernity that attracts both residents and visitors.

One of the defining features of Koreatown is its extensive array of restaurants and eateries, offering some of the best Korean cuisine outside of South Korea. From traditional Korean barbecue and hot pot to contemporary fusion dishes, Koreatown's dining options are vast and varied. Iconic spots like Kang Ho-dong Baekjeong and Quarters Korean BBQ are renowned for their high-quality meats and lively dining experiences. The neighborhood is also famous for its 24-hour restaurants, ensuring that visitors can enjoy delicious food at any hour.

In addition to its culinary delights, Koreatown boasts a dynamic nightlife scene. The neighborhood is home to numerous karaoke bars, nightclubs, and speakeasies, making it a popular destination for evening entertainment. Koreatown's karaoke bars, known as noraebangs, offer private rooms where groups can sing and party in a more intimate setting. Clubs like Arena Ktown and The Venue provide vibrant dance floors and top-tier DJs, drawing crowds for a night of dancing and fun.

Koreatown is also rich in cultural and recreational activities. The Wiltern Theatre, a historic Art Deco venue, hosts a variety of concerts, comedy shows, and events, adding to the neighborhood's cultural vibrancy. For those seeking relaxation, Koreatown's numerous Korean spas, or jjimjilbangs, offer luxurious treatments and traditional Korean wellness experiences.

The neighborhood's shopping scene is diverse, with a mix of traditional Korean markets, trendy boutiques, and modern malls. Koreatown Plaza and the MaDang Courtyard are popular shopping destinations that offer a variety of retail stores, eateries, and entertainment options.

Koreatown's architecture reflects its cultural diversity, with a blend of historic buildings and modern high-rises. The area is known for its vibrant street art and murals, which add to its colorful and dynamic atmosphere.

Community events and festivals play a significant role in Koreatown's cultural life. The annual Korean Festival features traditional performances, food stalls, and cultural exhibits, celebrating the rich heritage of the Korean community.

With its rich culinary offerings, vibrant nightlife, and cultural attractions, Koreatown provides a lively and immersive experience. Whether enjoying a delicious meal, exploring its entertainment options, or participating in cultural events, visitors to Koreatown are sure to be captivated by its dynamic and diverse character.

Westwood

Westwood, a bustling neighborhood on the west side of Los Angeles, is best known for being the home of the University of California, Los Angeles (UCLA). With its mix of academic vibrancy, historic landmarks, and cultural attractions, Westwood offers a lively and engaging environment that appeals to students, professionals, and visitors alike.

At the heart of Westwood is UCLA, one of the top public universities in the United States. The campus is a hub of activity, offering a wealth of cultural and educational opportunities. The UCLA Hammer Museum, located just off campus, is renowned for its impressive collection of contemporary art, as well as its dynamic programming, including exhibitions, lectures, and performances. The Fowler Museum at UCLA focuses on global arts and cultures, showcasing artifacts and exhibitions that span diverse cultures and historical periods.

Westwood Village, the commercial district adjacent to UCLA, is a vibrant area filled with shops, restaurants, and entertainment options. The village's historic theaters, such as the Fox Village Theatre and the Bruin Theatre, are iconic landmarks that host movie premieres and screenings, contributing to the neighborhood's lively atmosphere. The village also features an array of dining options, from casual eateries and coffee shops to upscale restaurants, catering to a wide range of tastes and preferences.

The neighborhood's historic charm is evident in its architecture, with many buildings dating back to the early 20th century. The Holmby Hills area, part of Westwood, is known for its luxurious homes and beautiful tree-lined streets, providing a glimpse into the neighborhood's affluent history.

Westwood's green spaces and recreational facilities offer residents and visitors opportunities for outdoor activities and relaxation. The Mildred E. Mathias Botanical Garden on the UCLA campus is a serene oasis with a diverse collection of plants from around the world. Westwood Park and the nearby Los Angeles National Cemetery provide additional green spaces for picnics, sports, and quiet reflection.

Cultural events and community activities play a significant role in Westwood's appeal. The neighborhood hosts various events throughout the year, including street fairs, farmers' markets, and cultural festivals that celebrate the diverse heritage of its residents.

With its blend of academic excellence, cultural attractions, and vibrant community life, Westwood offers a unique and enriching experience. Whether exploring the university campus, enjoying the amenities of Westwood Village, or participating in community events, visitors to Westwood are sure to appreciate its dynamic and welcoming atmosphere.

Arts District

The Arts District, located on the eastern edge of Downtown Los Angeles, is a vibrant and rapidly evolving neighborhood known for its thriving creative community, industrial-chic aesthetic, and diverse cultural offerings. Once a hub of manufacturing and warehouses, the Arts District has transformed into a dynamic area filled with art galleries, studios, trendy restaurants, and unique shops.

The neighborhood's artistic spirit is evident in its numerous galleries and creative spaces. The Hauser & Wirth gallery, housed in a sprawling industrial complex, is one of the district's premier art venues, featuring contemporary art exhibitions, a bookstore, and a garden. The district is also home to many smaller galleries and independent studios, where local artists and designers showcase their work. Street art and murals add to the district's vibrant visual landscape, with large-scale pieces by renowned artists decorating the walls of buildings throughout the area.

The Arts District's culinary scene is diverse and innovative, offering a wide range of dining options that reflect the neighborhood's creative energy. From artisanal coffee shops and gourmet food trucks to upscale restaurants and craft breweries, the area caters to a variety of tastes and preferences. Notable dining spots include Bestia, known for its Italian-inspired cuisine, and the Arts District Brewing Co., which offers a selection of craft beers brewed on-site.

The district's nightlife is equally lively, with a mix of bars, lounges, and live music venues providing ample entertainment options. Resident, a popular bar and music venue, hosts a variety of live performances, from indie bands to DJ sets, in an intimate outdoor setting. The district's rooftop bars, such as Upstairs at the Ace Hotel, offer stunning views of the downtown skyline and are perfect for a night out.

The Arts District is also home to unique shops and boutiques that reflect the neighborhood's creative ethos. From vintage clothing stores and design shops to artisanal markets and bookstores, the area offers a curated shopping experience that appeals to those looking for one-of-a-kind items.

Community events and cultural festivals play a significant role in the Arts District's vibrant atmosphere. The district hosts art walks, open studio events, and cultural celebrations that bring together residents and visitors to enjoy the area's creative offerings.

With its blend of artistic expression, culinary innovation, and cultural vibrancy, the Arts District offers a unique and immersive experience. Whether exploring its galleries, enjoying its diverse dining scene, or participating in community events, visitors to the Arts District are sure to be inspired by its dynamic and creative spirit.

Food and Dining

Iconic LA Foods

Los Angeles is famous for its diverse and innovative culinary scene, offering a wide array of iconic foods that reflect the city's multicultural heritage and creative spirit. From street tacos to In-N-Out burgers, and Korean BBQ, these quintessential LA eats are beloved by locals and tourists alike. Each of these foods has a unique history and place to find the best versions in the city.

Street Tacos

Street tacos are a staple of Los Angeles cuisine, known for their simplicity and burst of authentic flavors. Influenced by the city's rich Mexican heritage, street tacos are typically made with soft corn tortillas, filled with a variety of meats, and topped with fresh ingredients like cilantro, onions, and salsa.

Street tacos became popular in LA in the early 20th century, brought by Mexican immigrants who introduced the vibrant flavors of their homeland. Today, they can be found at numerous food trucks, taquerias, and street vendors across the city.

Some of the most famous spots for street tacos in Los Angeles include:

- **Guerilla Tacos:** Known for its gourmet approach to street tacos, Guerilla Tacos offers inventive fillings and top-quality ingredients.
- **Leo's Tacos Truck:** A beloved taco truck known for its al pastor tacos, cooked on a vertical spit and served with pineapple.
- **El Chato Taco Truck:** Popular for its late-night service and delicious carne asada and al pastor tacos.

In-N-Out Burgers

In-N-Out Burger is a fast-food icon that originated in Southern California and has become synonymous with LA's fast-food culture. Known for its fresh ingredients and simple menu, In-N-Out offers burgers, fries, and shakes that have garnered a cult following.

The first In-N-Out Burger stand opened in Baldwin Park, a suburb of LA, in 1948. Since then, it has expanded while maintaining its commitment to quality and consistency. The secret menu, including the famous "Animal Style" burger and fries, adds to its allure.

Notable In-N-Out Burger locations in Los Angeles:

- **In-N-Out Burger at Hollywood:** Located on Sunset Boulevard, this branch is popular with both locals and tourists.
- **In-N-Out Burger at LAX:** A favorite spot for travelers, offering a quintessential LA experience as soon as they arrive.
- **In-N-Out Burger at Westwood:** Near UCLA, this location is bustling with college students and Westside residents.

Korean BBQ

Korean BBQ has become a defining part of LA's culinary landscape, particularly in the neighborhood of Koreatown. This dining experience involves grilling marinated meats, such as beef, pork, and chicken, right at the table, accompanied by a variety of banchan (side dishes).

Korean immigrants introduced this interactive dining style to LA in the late 20th century, and it quickly gained popularity for its communal and flavorful experience.

Top spots for Korean BBQ in Los Angeles include:

- **Kang Ho Dong Baekjeong:** Known for its high-quality meats and vibrant atmosphere, this spot is a favorite among Korean BBQ enthusiasts.
- **Parks BBQ:** An upscale Korean BBQ restaurant renowned for its premium cuts and exceptional service.

- **Genwa Korean BBQ:** Offers an extensive menu and elegant setting, perfect for both casual dining and special occasions.

Hot Dogs

The Los Angeles hot dog scene is as diverse as the city itself, with a variety of styles and toppings that reflect its multicultural influences. From classic American hot dogs to the unique LA street-style "danger dog," wrapped in bacon and topped with grilled onions and peppers, there's something for everyone.

Popular hot dog spots in Los Angeles include:

- **Pink's Hot Dogs:** An LA institution since 1939, known for its celebrity-themed dogs and endless topping options.
- **Carney's:** Located in a vintage train car on Sunset Boulevard, Carney's serves up classic hot dogs and chili dogs that have been a favorite for decades.
- **Dog Haus:** A modern chain offering gourmet hot dogs with creative toppings and combinations, all served on King's Hawaiian rolls.

Each of these iconic foods—street tacos, In-N-Out burgers, Korean BBQ, and hot dogs—represents a slice of Los Angeles's rich culinary history and vibrant culture. Sampling these treats is not just about enjoying great food; it's about experiencing the diverse and dynamic flavors that make LA's food scene one of the most exciting in the world. Whether you're a local or a visitor, diving into these culinary delights offers a delicious way to connect with the city's unique identity.

Fine Dining

Los Angeles is home to some of the world's most renowned fine dining establishments, offering exquisite culinary experiences that attract food enthusiasts from around the globe. The city's fine dining scene is characterized by its diversity, innovation, and the sheer number of Michelin-starred restaurants.

Michelin-Starred Restaurants

Los Angeles boasts an impressive number of Michelin-starred restaurants, representing a wide array of cuisines and styles. These establishments are known for their meticulous attention to detail, exceptional service, and the use of the finest ingredients.

- **Providence:** A celebrated seafood restaurant by Chef Michael Cimarusti, Providence has maintained its two Michelin stars for many years. Known for its elegant, understated ambiance and perfectly executed dishes, it's a must-visit for seafood lovers.
- **n/naka:** This two Michelin-starred restaurant offers a modern take on kaiseki, a traditional Japanese multi-course meal. Chef Niki Nakayama's creative approach to fine dining has earned n/naka numerous accolades.
- **Melisse:** Located in Santa Monica, Chef Josiah Citrin's Melisse features a tasting menu that reflects his commitment to culinary excellence. The restaurant's intimate setting adds to the exceptional dining experience.

Internationally Inspired Fine Dining

Los Angeles's fine dining scene also includes a variety of internationally inspired restaurants that bring global flavors to the city.

- **Mori Sushi:** This Michelin-starred sushi restaurant by Chef Morihiro Onodera offers an omakase experience that is both intimate and luxurious. With fish flown in daily from Japan, Mori Sushi is considered one of the best sushi restaurants in the world.
- **Republique:** Chef Walter Manzke's flagship restaurant, Republique, offers French cuisine with a modern twist. The elegant setting and impeccable service make it a favorite among fine dining aficionados.
- **Jean-Georges Beverly Hills:** Situated in the Waldorf Astoria, Jean-Georges Vongerichten's eponymous restaurant features a menu that blends French, American, and Asian influences. The restaurant's innovative dishes and sophisticated atmosphere have earned it high praise.

Casual Eateries

Los Angeles's casual eateries offer a more relaxed dining experience without compromising on quality. From neighborhood bistros to trendy cafes, these establishments provide a diverse range of delicious and affordable options.

Neighborhood Favorites

Casual eateries are often neighborhood institutions, beloved by locals for their cozy ambiance and consistently good food.

- **Gjelina:** With its inviting atmosphere and Mediterranean-inspired menu, Gjelina in Venice is known for dishes like wood-fired pizzas and seasonal small plates.
- **Pizzana:** This Brentwood hotspot is famous for its Neapolitan-style pizzas and laid-back vibe. The menu also features a variety of creative salads and desserts.
- **Petit Trois:** A charming French bistro in Hollywood, Petit Trois offers a menu of simple yet delicious dishes like escargot, omelette, and steak frites. Its intimate setting makes it perfect for brunch or a casual dinner.

Trendy Cafes and Diners

Los Angeles is also home to a plethora of trendy cafes and diners that serve up everything from classic American fare to innovative brunch dishes.

- **Eggslut:** Located in Grand Central Market, Eggslut offers a menu of egg-centric dishes, including their famous Fairfax sandwich and the Slut, a coddled egg on potato purée.
- **The Griddle Cafe:** Known for its hearty breakfast and lunch options, The Griddle Cafe in Hollywood draws crowds for its massive pancakes, French toast, and unique omelets.

- **Blu Jam Cafe:** Famous for its crunchy French toast, Blu Jam Cafe in Melrose offers an all-day breakfast and comfort food menu that attracts locals and tourists alike.

Each of these fine dining and casual eateries represents a slice of Los Angeles's rich culinary scene. Sampling these establishments is not just about enjoying great food; it's about experiencing a piece of the city's vibrant culture and traditions. Whether you're looking for a luxurious dining experience or a cozy spot to enjoy a meal, LA's diverse food scene has something to offer everyone.

Street Food and Food Trucks

Los Angeles's street food and food truck scene is vibrant and diverse, offering a quick and delicious way to sample a wide range of cuisines. From taco trucks to gourmet food trucks, these mobile eateries are an integral part of the city's culinary landscape.

Classic Street Food

The city's classic street food vendors have become iconic symbols of Los Angeles's laid-back, diverse lifestyle. In addition to the already mentioned street tacos and hot dogs, street carts and food trucks in the city offer:

- **Bacon-Wrapped Hot Dogs:** Known as "danger dogs," these hot dogs are wrapped in bacon and typically topped with grilled onions, peppers, and jalapeños. They are a popular late-night snack, especially outside bars and clubs.

Gourmet Food Trucks

The city's food truck scene has exploded in recent years, with gourmet trucks offering inventive and high-quality dishes from around the world.

- **Kogi BBQ:** This pioneering food truck fuses Korean flavors with Mexican street food, serving up delicious dishes like Korean short rib tacos and kimchi quesadillas. Founded by Chef Roy Choi, Kogi BBQ sparked the gourmet food truck movement in LA.
- **Guerrilla Tacos:** Started by Chef Wes Avila, Guerrilla Tacos offers a creative take on traditional tacos, using high-quality, seasonal ingredients. Popular items include the sweet potato taco and the ahi tuna tostada.
- **The Lobos Truck:** Known for its indulgent comfort food, The Lobos Truck offers dishes like mac and cheese fries, buffalo chicken sandwiches, and gourmet burgers.
- **Coolhaus:** A favorite for dessert lovers, Coolhaus serves architecturally inspired ice cream sandwiches with unique flavors like brown butter candied bacon ice cream and chocolate chipotle cookies.

Ethnic Cuisine

Los Angeles is a global melting pot, and nowhere is this more evident than in its diverse neighborhoods, each offering a rich tapestry of ethnic cuisines. Little Tokyo, Thai Town, and Koreatown are three of the most vibrant areas, where visitors can indulge in authentic and delicious foods from around the world.

Little Tokyo

Little Tokyo, located in Downtown Los Angeles, is a historic district that celebrates the legacy of Japanese immigrants who settled in the city in the early 20th century. The area is known for its rich cultural heritage and vibrant culinary scene, offering a taste of Japan in the heart of LA.

- **Sushi:** Sushi Gen and Sushi Komasa are renowned for their fresh and authentic sushi offerings, attracting sushi lovers from all over the city.
- **Ramen:** Daikokuya and Shin-Sen-Gumi Hakata Ramen are popular spots for enjoying hearty bowls of ramen.

- **Japanese Sweets:** Mikawaya offers traditional Japanese sweets, including mochi ice cream, while Fugetsu-Do, one of the oldest family-owned Japanese confectioneries in the U.S., is famous for its mochi and manju.

Little Tokyo also features various cultural institutions like the Japanese American National Museum and the Little Tokyo Galleria, making it a cultural and culinary destination.

Thai Town

Thai Town, located in East Hollywood, is the first officially recognized Thai Town in the United States. Established in the 1990s, this vibrant neighborhood offers an array of authentic Thai cuisine and cultural experiences.

- **Authentic Thai Cuisine:** Jitlada is famous for its Southern Thai specialties and spicy dishes, while Pa Ord Noodle offers delicious boat noodles and other Thai street food favorites.
- **Thai Desserts:** Bhan Kanom Thai is a popular dessert shop offering traditional Thai sweets like mango sticky rice, Thai iced tea, and pandan waffles.
- **Cultural Experience:** Thai Town also hosts the annual Songkran Festival, celebrating the Thai New Year with traditional music, dance, and food.

Koreatown

Koreatown, located in Central Los Angeles, is a bustling neighborhood known for its Korean restaurants, bakeries, and nightlife. Often referred to as "K-town," this area offers an immersive experience of Korean culture and cuisine.

- **Korean BBQ:** Koreatown is renowned for its Korean BBQ restaurants, where diners can grill their own meat at the table. Popular spots include Kang Ho Dong Baekjeong and Park's BBQ, where guests can enjoy a variety of marinated meats, seafood, and vegetables cooked over a charcoal grill.

- **Soondubu Jjigae:** BCD Tofu House is famous for its bubbling hot pots of soondubu jjigae (soft tofu stew), offering a comforting and flavorful dining experience.
- **Homestyle Korean Dishes:** Sun Nong Dan is known for its galbi jjim (braised short ribs), while Hangari Kalguksu serves delicious handmade knife-cut noodle soups.

Koreatown's food scene extends beyond savory dishes to include an array of sweet treats and beverages. Paris Baguette and Tous Les Jours are popular Korean bakeries that offer a delightful selection of pastries, cakes, and bread. For a refreshing dessert, visitors can try bingsu, a Korean shaved ice dessert topped with fruits, condensed milk, and sweet red beans, at places like Oakobing.

In addition to its culinary delights, Koreatown is known for its vibrant nightlife. Karaoke bars, or noraebang, such as Palm Tree LA, offer a fun and lively atmosphere where groups can sing their favorite songs in private rooms.

Boyle Heights

Boyle Heights is a historic neighborhood known for its rich Mexican-American heritage. It offers an array of authentic Mexican cuisine and vibrant cultural experiences.

- **Mexican Cuisine:** La Serenata de Garibaldi is famous for its seafood dishes, while Guisados offers delicious tacos filled with slow-cooked stews.
- **Street Food:** Mariachi Plaza is a popular spot for street vendors selling tamales, elotes (grilled corn), and other Mexican street foods.
- **Panaderias (Bakeries):** El Aguila Bakery offers traditional Mexican pastries like conchas, pan dulce, and tres leches cake.

Boyle Heights also hosts cultural events and festivals that celebrate its Mexican heritage, making it a must-visit for those looking to experience authentic Mexican culture in LA.

Sawtelle Japantown

Located on the Westside of Los Angeles, Sawtelle Japantown is a vibrant neighborhood known for its Japanese and Asian-inspired cuisine. The area, often referred to as "Little Osaka," is packed with restaurants, cafes, and shops.

- **Ramen:** Tsujita LA and Daikokuya offer some of the best ramen bowls in the city, with rich broths and perfectly cooked noodles.
- **Sushi:** Hide Sushi and Kiriko Sushi are popular spots for fresh, high-quality sushi.
- **Asian Fusion:** ROC offers delicious Taiwanese dumplings, while Seoul Sausage serves Korean-inspired sausages and street food.

Sawtelle Japantown also features unique shops and dessert spots, such as Blockheads Shavery for snow cream and B Sweet Dessert Bar for decadent sweets.

Little Tokyo, Thai Town, Koreatown, Boyle Heights, and Sawtelle Japantown each provide a unique culinary journey, showcasing the rich traditions and flavors of their respective cultures. Exploring these neighborhoods offers a delicious and immersive experience of Los Angeles's diverse food scene. Whether you're craving sushi, spicy Thai dishes, Korean BBQ, Mexican street food, or Asian fusion cuisine, LA's ethnic enclaves offer something to satisfy every palate.

Food Markets

Los Angeles is renowned for its diverse culinary landscape, and its food markets are some of the best places to experience this gastronomic variety. Among these, Grand Central Market and Smorgasburg LA stand out as must-visit destinations for food lovers seeking a wide array of flavors and culinary delights.

Grand Central Market

Located in Downtown Los Angeles at 317 S Broadway, Grand Central Market is one of the city's most iconic indoor food markets. Established in 1917, the market has retained much of its historic charm while evolving into a bustling hub for food enthusiasts. With its eclectic mix of vendors, Grand Central Market offers a vibrant snapshot of LA's diverse culinary scene.

Grand Central Market is a food lover's paradise, featuring a wide range of vendors that cater to various tastes and preferences. Visitors can find everything from artisanal bread and fresh produce to gourmet sandwiches and exotic spices. Popular vendors include:

- **Eggslut:** Known for its delectable egg sandwiches, Eggslut attracts long lines of eager customers.
- **Wexler's Deli:** Famous for its traditional Jewish deli offerings, including pastrami on rye and smoked fish platters.
- **Sari Sari Store:** Offering Filipino comfort food, this spot is beloved for dishes like sisig and halo-halo.

In addition to its food stalls, Grand Central Market features several sit-down restaurants where visitors can enjoy a full meal. **Belcampo Meat Co.** offers high-quality, sustainably sourced meats, while **Golden Road Brewing** serves craft beers and pub fare. The market also houses retail shops selling kitchenware, specialty foods, and unique gifts, making it a one-stop destination for both culinary delights and shopping.

Smorgasburg LA

Smorgasburg LA, often referred to as "the Woodstock of eating," is an open-air food market that showcases some of the best street food vendors in Los Angeles. Founded in 2016, Smorgasburg LA has become a beloved weekend tradition, drawing thousands of visitors to its location at ROW DTLA.

The market operates year-round, every Sunday, featuring over 100 local vendors offering an incredible variety of dishes, from classic comfort foods to innovative culinary creations. Notable vendors include:

- **Lobsterdamus:** Known for its mouthwatering lobster dishes, including lobster fries and grilled lobster tails.
- **Todo Verde:** Offering plant-based Mexican-inspired dishes, Todo Verde is famous for its tacos and agua frescas.
- **Shrimp Daddy:** A hit for its Hawaiian garlic butter shrimp served in pineapple bowls.

One of the highlights of Smorgasburg LA is the opportunity to sample a diverse array of international cuisines all in one place. Visitors can enjoy everything from Japanese-inspired tacos and Venezuelan arepas to Filipino halo-halo and Italian gelato. The market's lively atmosphere, combined with its scenic downtown location, makes it a perfect spot for a leisurely weekend outing.

The Original Farmers Market

Located at 6333 W 3rd Street, adjacent to The Grove shopping center, The Original Farmers Market has been an LA institution since 1934. This historic market offers a delightful mix of old-world charm and contemporary food offerings, making it a favorite destination for both locals and tourists.

- **Bob's Coffee & Doughnuts:** Famous for its classic doughnuts and freshly brewed coffee, a perfect spot for a morning treat.
- **Monsieur Marcel:** A French market and bistro offering an array of gourmet cheeses, charcuterie, and French dishes.
- **Lotería Grill:** Known for its authentic Mexican cuisine, including tacos, enchiladas, and guacamole.

In addition to its food vendors, The Original Farmers Market features specialty shops selling everything from fresh produce and meats to handcrafted gifts and souvenirs. The market's charming, open-air setting provides a relaxed atmosphere for exploring and indulging in a variety of culinary delights.

Both Grand Central Market and Smorgasburg LA offer unique and memorable culinary experiences, showcasing the best of Los Angeles's vibrant food scene. Whether you're exploring the historic indoor market of Grand Central or indulging in the diverse street food offerings at Smorgasburg, these food markets are essential destinations for any food enthusiast visiting the city. The Original Farmers Market adds another layer of history and variety, making LA a true haven for food lovers.

Made in United States
North Haven, CT
08 January 2025